Andrew Wright

Court-Hand Restored

The Student's Assistant in Reading Old Deeds, Charters, Records etc.

Andrew Wright

Court-Hand Restored
The Student's Assistant in Reading Old Deeds, Charters, Records etc.

ISBN/EAN: 9783337117887

Printed in Europe, USA, Canada, Australia, Japan

Cover: Foto ©Suzi / pixelio.de

More available books at **www.hansebooks.com**

Court-Hand Restored

OR, THE

STUDENT'S ASSISTANT

IN READING

Old Deeds, Charters, Records, etc.

NEATLY ENGRAVED ON TWENTY-THREE COPPER-PLATES,

DESCRIBING

The Old Law Hands, with their Contractions and Abbreviations.

WITH AN APPENDIX

CONTAINING

The Ancient Names of Places in Great Britain and Ireland;

AN ALPHABETICAL TABLE OF ANCIENT SURNAMES;

AND

A GLOSSOGRAPHY OF LATIN WORDS FOUND IN THE WORKS OF THE
MOST EMINENT LAWYERS, AND OTHER ANCIENT WRITINGS,

BUT NOT IN ANY MODERN DICTIONARIES;

A WORK NOT ONLY USEFUL TO REMIND THE LEARNED, BUT ADSOLUTELY NECESSARY FOR YOUNG STUDENTS, AND
OTHERS, WHO HAVE OCCASION TO CONSULT OLD CHARTERS, DEEDS, OR RECORDS.

By ANDREW WRIGHT,

OF THE INNER TEMPLE.

THE EIGHTH EDITION, CORRECTED.

LONDON:
HENRY G. BOHN, 4 YORK STREET, COVENT GARDEN.
M.DCCC.LXIV.

LONDON:
STRANGEWAYS AND WALDEN, PRINTERS, 28 Castle St. Leicester Sq.

INTRODUCTION

FIRST EDITION.

ALTHOUGH it is universally agreed that the public have reaped some advantages by the Acts of the 4th Geo. II. c. 26, and 6th Geo. II. c. 14, requiring all Law-Pleadings, Deeds, &c. to be thereafter written in English, yet the Tax growing from those advantages is become so excessive, that few persons are now to be found capable of reading or explaining old Deeds and Charters, with any satisfaction to themselves or others.

This great inconvenience must have arisen from the Acts above mentioned; for, it being vainly imagined that, after the passing of those Acts, Court-Hand and Latin were unnecessary accomplishments for a Lawyer, young gentlemen were frequently articled to Attorneys and Solicitors without the knowledge of either; and even called to the Bar without learning to read the Court-Hand or the Abbreviations of it. The inconveniences brought on by this neglect were in some measure salved *pro tempore* by Old Practitioners then living, who were in business when the Law-Pleadings were in Latin, and were familiar with the contractions; but time having gradually deprived the Law of those valuable Gentlemen of the profession, I believe it may with truth and modesty, be affirmed, from the numerous applications that are made to me on that subject, that the Reading of the old Law-Hands is at this day very nearly (if not altogether) become obsolete, though useful. I make this declaration with some
concern;

concern ; for although it is not necessary as the Law now stands, to *write* the Court or any other of the old Law-Hands, yet, as Records written in those hands are daily produced in Evidence in the Courts of Law, the being able to *read* them with propriety and certainty cannot be an unnecessary accomplishment, not only for young Students, Stewards of Manors, and others, but also for the most dignified characters in the profession, as in cases of Quo Warrantos and Election Business, Records and old Charters are almost constantly referred to ; and he who best understands the Abbreviations, bids fairest for a true explanation of the matter in question. Gentlemen of liberal education and large property might, perhaps, not find it disadvantageous to be acquainted with old writings, as by that means they would be enabled to preserve the large Honors, Manors, Royalties, and Demesnes, descended to them from their Noble Ancestors, which are too often liable to be encroached upon by designing men, and not be reduced to the necessity of taking upon trust the declarations of some of the profession, who call every old Deed useless, because they do not understand it, though the old writing, treated with this amazing ignorance and temerity, may be a material Title Deed of a very ancient and extensive Manor, or Lordship, or part thereof. Nor would the knowledge of the Old Hands, as I humbly conceive, be unacceptable to the learned Historian, who, when in search of materials to authenticate his productions, would be able (especially as the Law Contractions are well known to be in some degree in imitation of the old Monkish writers) to examine his Copies with the *Records themselves*, and not depend entirely upon the Copying Clerk, who might, by an error in transcribing, lose the true meaning of the original,—an event equally dangerous to truth, property, and to liberty itself.

Many young gentlemen of the Law, whose studies are much interrupted by large fortunes, and perhaps a natural gaiety of disposition, will, I make no doubt, in order to palliate their inattention to the knowledge now contended for, say, that numbers of the Records in the kingdom have been copied into the Works of many learned men, and therefore are as good evidence as the originals :

ginals : in this I must beg leave to differ, and to remind the learned of the following Cases (amongst others), wherein Camden's "Britannia," Sir William Dugdale's "Baronage," and "Monasticon," although valuable productions, were refused to be admitted as Evidence.

1. Camden's "Britannia" was offered in evidence to prove a particular Custom, but refused ; for the Court was of opinion that a general History was not sufficient to prove a particular right or custom.

2. In Ejectment for the Barony of Cockermouth, and all the other Estates of Joceline, formerly Earl of Northumberland, the Lessor shewed an Inquisition in the time of Richard the IInd. which found an entail on the then Earl of Northumberland, and the heirs male of his body, and derived his Title from Sir Inglaram Piercy, the second son of Henry the fifth Earl of Northumberland of that name, and offered in evidence the "Baronage of England," written by Sir William Dugdale, King-at-Arms, but refused.—Sir Thomas Jones's Reports, 164. *Piercy against* ————.

3. It being a question in the Exchequer, whether the Abbey de Sentibus was an inferior Abbey or not, Dugdale's "Monasticon" was produced for Evidence, and refused, because the original Records might have been had in the Augmentation-Office.—1 *Salkeld*, 281. 7th Wm. III. Stainer and the Burgesses of Droitwich.—See also *Skinner*, 624.

4. On a trial at Bar for lands in Com. York, upon Ejectment, the Lessor of the Plaintiff made out his title under a gift in tail made by Richard the IInd. to Robert de Clifford and the heirs of his body, and, in order to prove himself heir of the body of the said Robert, he produced a Pedigree by which the descent appeared : Sir William Dugdale and other Heralds being sworn, declared that the Pedigree had been deduced out of *Records* and *ancient Books* in the Heralds' Office ; but the Court would not allow that for evidence, without

shewing the Records and Books from whence it had been extracted; and afterwards they produced *an ancient book* ending in the year 1582, which was allowed for evidence, and confirmed the Pedigree.—*King against Foster.* Sir Thomas Jones' Reports, fo. 224.

From all which it may be reasonably concluded, that although the works of those great men are highly beneficial to consult in the *first instance*, yet, where there is a possibility of producing the original Record, the Court always requires the best evidence that the nature of the Case will admit, and therefore it is highly necessary that all Gentlemen of the Law should be able to read them in their original state.

In order to attain this end, and to avoid the prolixity and inconvenience that must attend the giving separate Tables or Plates for the Contractions of each particular Hand, I have pitched upon the *Court-Hand* and *its Contractions*, as the best and most difficult of the Old Law-Hands; a perfect knowledge of which will, with a little application, soon gain absolute dominion over the rest.

The 1st and 2d Plates contain large Court-Hand Alphabets, with some Contractions; and in Plates 3d and 4th will be found the Chancery-Hand, and small Court-Hand Alphabets, with specimens of both. The Alphabetical Contractions of the Court-Hand will be found in Plates 5th, 6th, and 7th; and Christian Names, as they have been usually contracted, in Plates 8th and 9th; and such Words as were commonly contracted in old Charters, &c. Plates 10 to 15 inclusive. The counties of England and Wales, and also the Bishops of England, in the manner they are usually written in old Records, in Plates 16th and 17th. And, lastly, a General Alphabet, with Specimens of very ancient Charters, Deeds, &c. Plates 18, 19, and 20. All which are collected from Manuscripts in my own possession, and the Contractions made as I really found them in the different originals from whence they are extracted. The reason

of

of my introducing a general Alphabet is, because many of the ancient Writings differ extremely from the Court and Chancery Hands. The different Characters are therefore here placed in one view; and if the Letter in doubt cannot be found in the Alphabets of the Court and Chancery Hands, it is more than probable it will appear in the general Alphabet, No. 18 or 19.

ANDREW WRIGHT.

Barnard's Inn, *March* 1773.

FOURTH EDITION.

To this Edition are added Copper Plates, exhibiting the various Hands in use from the time of William the Conqueror to that of Queen Elizabeth, from the Collection of the late Thomas Astle, Esq. with Explanations by John Caley, Esq. which cannot be better introduced than by the following Abstracts from Returns made by Mr. Astle and Mr. Caley to the Special Orders of the Select Committee on the Public Records of the Kingdom.

FIFTH EDITION.

To this Edition is also added an Explanation of the Contractions used in Printing the Records and Manuscripts copied in the Works printed under the direction of the Commissioners of Public Records.

From

From the Return of THOMAS ASTLE, ESQ. *Keeper of the Records in the Tower of London.*

" THE Characters which were introduced into this country by King William I. were at that time called Lombardic, but soon afterwards they acquired the appellation of Norman Characters, which were generally used in Grants, Charters, Public Instruments, and Law Proceedings, with very little alteration from that period until the Reign of King Edward III. In that of King Richard II. variations took place in Hand-Writings of Records and Law Proceedings ; the Characters used from that Time to the Reign of King Henry VIII. are composed partly of Characters called Set Chancery and Common Chancery, and of some of the Letters called Court-Hand. The Chancery Letters were used for all Records which passed the Great Seal; the Court-Hand in the Courts of King's Bench and Common Pleas, for Fines, Placita, Adjudicata, &c. These latter Characters came into general Use about the middle of the 16th Century, and were continued until the beginning of the late Reign, when they were entirely disused ; they were originally the Lombardic or Norman, but corrupted and deformed to so great a degree, that they bore very little resemblance to their prototypes. In the 16th Century the English Lawyers engrossed their Conveyances and Legal Instruments in Characters called Secretary, which are still in use.

" Many Grants and Charters, especially those written by the Monks, were in Letters called Modern Gothic, which took place in England in the 12th Century.

" From the latter End of the 13th to the 17th Century, our Lawyers, when they wrote in the English Language, made use of Characters which were derived from the modern Gothic ; these were generally used by them for Conveyances, Wills, &c. until about the Middle of the 17th Century. I think the Set Chancery the most durable, and therefore the most proper to be used in future for Patents, Charters, &c."

From

From the Return of JOHN CALEY, ESQ. *Keeper of the Records in the Augmentation Office.*

" The Character or Hand-writing of ancient Records, as far as my observation has extended, has gradually degenerated from Age to Age; thus the Records of the Saxon Era, whether written in Saxon or Latin, are infinitely more plain and legible than those of subsequent Eras; they are also little obscured with Abbreviations, which have created much Doubt and Ambiguity in after-ages, particularly in that valuable Record Domesday Book.

" From the Norman Conquest until the Reign of Henry III. the Character is in general plain and perspicuous; of this latter Reign, however, there are many Records which cannot be read with facility, on account of the Intricacy of the Character, and the Number of Abbreviations.

" The same Observations may be applied to Records from this Reign until that of Edward III. inclusive.

" From this Period downwards, I have experimentally found that less Difficulty occurs in reading and translating Records, and that the Hands used from the Reign of Richard II. to that of Philip and Mary are such as may be read without much Trouble.

" Hitherto each Reign appears to have had a set or uniform Character; but in the Reign of Elizabeth and her Successors, the Clerical Mode seems to have been in a great Measure abandoned, and each Transcriber to have written according to his own Fancy; and it is observable that the English Records of the 16th and 17th Centuries are in general more difficult to be read than the Latin Records of preceding Ages.

B

" Ample

" Ample and accurate Specimens of the Characters used in all the Periods of English History may be seen in Mr. Astle's valuable Work on the Origin and Progress of Writing, to which I therefore beg leave to refer, as also to Madox's Formulare Anglicanum, and Casley's Catalogue of the MSS. in the King's Library."

The Publisher has availed himself of the researches of later Antiquaries, to render the List of the Names of Places in the Appendix more correct than in the former Editions.

Explanation of the Contractions used in Printing the Records and Manuscripts copied in the Works printed under the direction of the Commissioners of Public Records.

" WITH respect to the Printed Contractions, it is to be observed, that wherever the Manuscript is abbreviated, the Print has a Mark of Contraction, as similar to that of the Manuscript as the types will admit. The following Explanation of the Marks of Contraction used in the Print, may serve as well to render the Printed Copy intelligible, as also to explain the Contractions in the Manuscripts, and to make the reading and consulting of them, when necessary, more easy to Persons not used to Ancient Records.

A Straight Line over a Vowel denotes the omission of the Letter m or n following.

antiq⁴	antiquam
cōmun	commun
hōͤu	hominum
nō	non
quā	quam
statī	statim
volūtatē	voluntatem
avaūdiz	avaunditz

The Straight Line over m̄ in the middle of a Word denotes the omission of the Letter m or n following.

om̄es	omnes
om̄ia	omnia

A Crooked line over some Letter, or a Line through some Letter of the Word contracted, denotes the omission of one or more Letters of the Word.

Ballis	Ballivis
coronacõis	coronacionis

c̃o, tõ	cio or tio / cion or tion
dicī	dictum
Dͤus	Dominus
Eͤpis	Episcopis
expeditacõ	expeditacio
Gͤra	Gratia
ħeat	habeat
libͤtates	libertates
malicõse	maliciose
noͤb	nobis
oͤus or oīes	omnes
Salī	Salutem

A small Superior Letter denotes an omission of which such Letter forms a part.

impⁱsonetʳ	imprisonetur
occ°one	occasione
pⁱmis	primis
pⁱ⁹	prius
nⁱ	nisi
sⁱ	sibi
qᵃm	} quam
qᵃ	

———

" The following CHARACTERS *or* ABBREVIATIONS *have certain explicit*
Significations, viz.

Character.	Signification.	
		At the End of Words in the Dative or Ablative Plural :
3	us sometimes } et	abbatib3 - - - abbatibus ‖ quib3 - - - - quibus s3 - - - - - set (sed) ‖ poss3 - - - - posset
		Or as a comprehensive Mark of Abbreviation :
		quil3 - - - quilibet ‖ videl3 - - - videlicet qn3 - - - quandoque ‖
9 above the Line.	us sometimes os, *or* ost	{huj9modi -} {h9ī - - -} } hujusmodi ‖ dedim9 - - - dedimus huj9 - - - hujus p9 {p9t } post ‖ p9tea - - - postea
9 even with the Line.	com, *or* con	{ęntenta - - contenta ‖ 9scil - - - - conscil {ęmuni - - communi
q̄ *or* q̖	que	absq̖ - - - absque ‖ usq̄ - - - - usque *Frequently used also for* quod *and* quia.
ꝗ ꝗ	er sometimes re	{eꝗcitum - - exercitum ‖ deꝰs - - - - deners {itiꝫe - - - itinere ‖ maꝫo - - - - manere {infreꝗint - infregerint ‖ eꝗssum - - egressum ‖ transꝗssum- transgressum
ꝝ	rum	antecessoꝝ - antecessorum ‖ nr̃oꝝ - - - nostrorum *Sometimes to mark an Abbreviation beginning with* r : coꝝ - - - - - coronacionem

&	et	{ *The* & *appears in the Print wherever an Abbreviation for* et *appears in the Manuscript.*

`t	and
&̃	eciam
÷	est

In the Copies of some Scotch Records.

c̃	cer	fec̃it - - -	fecerit	c̃tum - - -	certum
m̃	mer	am̃cietur -	amercietur	m̃cator - -	mercator
ſ̃	ser	ſ̃vicium - -	servicium	ſ̃vir - - -	servir
ꞇ	ter	cet̃a - - -	cetera	ꞇram - - -	terram
	sometimes				
	tre	ꞇ̃spasours -	trespasours		
ũ	uer	fũit - - -	fuerit	hũit - - -	habuerit
ꝟ	ver	estoꝟiũ - -	estoverium	oꝟtes - - -	overtes

ꝑ	per	} *As the Prepositions* per *and* pro, *and in forming Words :*
ꝑ	pro	}

		cepit - - -	ceperit	ꝑp'a - - -	propria
		ꝑbũ - - -	probum	psone - - -	persone
		aptement -	apertement	ꝑfit - - -	profit
		ꝑmisit - -	permisit	ꝑmisit - - -	promisit
		ꝑchein - -	prochein	pᷓ - - - -	persona
	also for				
ꝓ	par *and* por	patus - -	paratus	pceles - - -	parceles
		tempe - -	tempore	corpum - -	corporum
ꝓ	pre	ꝓsentem -	presentem	ꝓlaz - - -	prelatz
		ꝓdem - -	predictum	pndront - -	prendront

z	tz	fiz - - -	fitz	fcz - - -	fetz
		establisemenz -	establisementz	tenaunz -	tenauntz

In the Copies of some Records the following Characters occur :

ꝭ	is *or* s	Scottꝭ -	Scottis	*As also the Saxon Characters.*	
		Lordꝭ -	Lords	p - - th ꝥ ᵹ - - y	
ꜩ	et	ꜩc - - -	et cetera		
ꝼ	si, serim, *or* sis	geñoꝼ -	generosi, generoserim *or* generosis		
	bus	comꝼ -	comitatibus		

"In citing the several Statute Rolls, Parliament Rolls, and Close, Patent, Fine, and Charter Rolls, the Year of the King, the Part, if there are more Rolls than one of the same Year, the Membrane or Skin, and the Number of the Article, where it is so distinguished on the Roll, are particularised ; and if it is on the Dorse or Back of the Roll, that also is noticed. The several Membranes or Skins of which the Rolls are composed are frequently numbered from the bottom to the top of the Roll, the Membrane at the end being numbered 1, and so progressively up to the beginning of the Roll :—thus

Mag. Rot. Stat. m. 46 *d.* signifies { The Great Roll of the Statutes, or the back of Membrane 46.

Rot. Parl. 6 *Edw.* II. p. 2. *nu.* 3. { Parliament Roll 6 Edward II. Part II. Number 3.

Rot. Claus.   Close Roll.

Rot. Pat.   Patent Roll.

Rot. Fin.   Fine Roll.

Rot. Cart.   Charter Roll.

In Cedula.   In a Schedule or separate Skin or Membrane attached to the Roll."

A a B b C c D d E e F f G g

Court Hand Plate 2.

Plate 3

Sett Chancery Hand.

A Hand much used in the Reign of Ja.^s I.st

Jacobus dei gra Anglie. Scotie ffrancie
z Hibnie. Rex fidei defensor et Omnib3
ad quos psentes lie puenint Saltm.
Sciatis qd nos de gra nra Spiali ac
p octagint sex solid z octo denar. &c.

6.^{lb}. 16. i.^d

PLATE III.

Jacobus Dei gratia Anglie Scotie Francie
& Hibernie Rex Fidei Defensor, &c. Omnibus
ad quos presentes Littere pervenerint Salutem
Sciatis quod Nos de gratia nostra speciali ac
pro octaginta sex Solidis & octo Denarijs, &c.

Anno 6 Jac. I.

c

plate 1.

Chancery Hand

Small Court Hand.

PLATE IV.

Omnibus ad quos presentes littere pervenerint Salutem
Sciatis quod Nos de gratia nostra speciali ac ex certa
scientia & mero motu nostris, &c.

Humfridus Connyngton nuper de Londini Armiger summonitus fuit ad
respondendum Emmanueli Somerby Militi de placito quod
reddat ei centum & quinque libras quas ei debet &
injuste detinet, &c. Et unde idem E. &c.

Omnibus ad quos presentes littere pervenerint Salutem
Sciatis quod nos de gratia nostra speciali ac ex
certa scientia et mero motu concessimus.

Plate 5.

Contractions of the Court Hand.
The Syllables following are usually Abbreviated.

Armiger.

ber, bus.

cer, cerhum, cetera.

di, do, dum.

ger, gra.

mer — mus.

ner

per, pra, pre, pro.

quem, quam, que, quorta,

rus, rum.

ter, tra, tur.

ver

ser, us.

um.

fio tio &c.

xer.

gra, pra, tra.

These Syllables following are usually contracted at the beginning and middle of words.

ber — Libertus Gilbertus.

cer — certus, liceret, doceri.

gra — gratis, graviter, Rogerus.

mer — mercator, meruit.

ner — vulneravit, amerciamentum

per — percussit, superius.

pre — premissa, predictus.

pro — protulit, prout, prope.

ter — terra, terrarum, mitteret

fio ttio — proclamationem

tra — Transgressio, inhavit, extra.

ver — versus, diversas, verberavit.

Plate 6.

Contractions of the Court Hand continued.

These Syllables are usually abbreviated at the End of
  Words.

bus   quibus, quibuscunque.

di. do. dum.   habendum, interloquendi.

per.   semper, nuper, super.

pra   supra, infra, ultra.

quam   præterquam, quamvis.

que   quicunque, dictique.

quam   aliquam, quemlibet.

quod   quodlibet.

rum   futurus.

sio. tio.   versio, oratio, relatio.

ter   breviter, inter, fiter, propter.

tur   queritur, fiscitur, igitur.

um   mefuagium, aurum.

us

Gulielmus, precipimus, cujus, hujus &c.

Plate 7.

Alphabetical Contractions of the Court-Hand.

unam Vaccam, gratia &c.

nobis, vrbis, octabis.

vicecomes, dicit Justiciarius.

defendit, predictus, per omnes Casus.

venire facias, breve.

defendens, Sufficiens.

plegii de proſequendo.

attachiatus fuit.

Episcopi, niſi prius.

culpabilis, illa, Anglia, fidelis.

Weſtmonaſterium, Summonitus fuit.

venit per attornatum.

ponit loco ſuo, Ideo.

ſupra

Cumque etiam,

propria, Curia, Injuria &c.

conſideratio, ſimiſer, miſis, viſis.

requiſitus, priſatus, &c.

unam Meſuagium

ſit proximus per omnes Caſus.

or yeom for Yeoman.

videlicet, Merchandize &c.

plate 8.

Christian Names Contracted.

Abrus ~ Abrahamus, so *Abrñ.* *Abro.* *Abrum* .

Alexij ~ Alexander, so *Alexji.* *Alexjo.* *Alexjum.*

Andr ~ Andreas per omnes Casus .

Anthus ~ Anthonius, so *Anthi.* *Antho.* *Anthum.*

Baptra ~ Baptista . *Baptro* . Baptistæ &c .

Bathus . Bartholomeus, so *Bathi.* *Batho.* *Bathum.*

Beniamin ~ Benjaminus per omnes Casus .

Benedtus ~ Benedictus, *Benedñ.* *Benedto.* &c

Xtoferus . Christopherus, *Xtoferi.* *Xtofero.* &c

David ~ David &c omnes Casus &c so of other Hebrew Names .

Edus ~ Edmundus, so *Edñ* *Edo* *Edum* .

Edus ~ Edwardus *Edñ.* *Edo.* *Edum.*

Elizabeth ~ Elizabetha in Omnibus

Francus . Franciscus *Franci* *Franco* *Francum* .

Galfus ~ Galfridus *Galfi.* *Galfo.* *Galfum.*

Gilbtus ~ Gilbertus *Gilbti* &c

Godfus ~ Godfridus . *Godfi.* *Godfo.* &c

Humphus or *Humfus* ~ Humfridus &c

Plate 9.

Christian Names continued

Iohes. Iohannes. so

mittis. Michaelis. so

Richus. Nicholaus. so

Phus. Philippus. so

Ricus. Ricardus. so

Robtus. Robertus. so

Stophus. Stephanus. so

Waltus. Walterus. so

Willmus. Gulielmus or Wilhelmus.

Wilfrus. Wilfridus. so

Set Court Hands

PLATE IX.

Elizabeth Dei gratia Anglic Francie & Hibernie
Regina Fidei Defensor, &c.   Omnibus ad quos
presentes littere nostre pervenerint Salutem.   Sciatis
quod Robertus Donnington in Curia nostra coram
Justiciarijs nostris apud Westmonasterium implacitavit Robertum
Hammerton et Margeriam Uxorem ejus de, &c.

Plate 10.

A. / Words comonly contracted in Old Charters, &c

Abbía, = Abbatia &c. ADS, Ad sectam.

Aíarz, animarum. Als, alias. Agthus Archangelus.

Archiepus, Archiepiscopus. Appoit, appositus. &c.

Ar Armiger Assess, Asessatus. Assign, asignatus.

Assisa asisa. Assid, asidunt &c.

Attorn, = Attornatus &c. Attting, attingunt &c

B

Balliú, Balliva. Balltius, Balltium.

Barz. Baronettus. Billa Billa. Bon, bonus &c.

Btus beatus, Bte, Bto, Bto, Btum.

Bve or Bve, breve. Bpus, Bpr, Bpter, Bpatum, Bpibz.

C

Clicus, Clericus, Clici, Clico, Clicum, Clicorz.

Claum, Clausum. Cltm, Cto, Clus.

Cois communis, cou, coom, cooes, coibz.

Comptum, computum, compus, compar compus

Cons, confideratum.. Cstm, craftinum, Cstr, &c

Cur Curia, per omnes Casus. —

Plate II.

Words comonly contracted in Old Charters &c continued

D.

Dñus Dominus, Dñi, Dño, Dñm Dñon .

Dcbus or Dñs, dictus, Dcs, Dco, Dcm, Dcon, Dcr.

Dcbtum, debitum, Dcbi, Dcbo, Dcbon, Dcbis .

Dcfclis defectus Dcffu, defechim .

Dilcus dilectus, Dilcu, Dilco, Dilcim .

Dñibo, Dominico hcanu Dñicobom .

E.

Ecclia, Ecclesia, Effcus Effectus. &c

Eid eidem, Examabr examinatur .

Expositr eximpositus Excor Executor & Excutio

F.

fcus, factus &c. flls falsus, feod feodum .

frls fratris, frcim, frlo, frls, fluim, fribz .

G.

Gauus, Gavisus Genus, generosus .

Generabl generalis gbis grahis .

Gla gratia gue grave

~ **H.** ~

Plate 12.

Words comonly contracted in Old Charters &c. continued.

hēats, habeas, hot hōus, hēnt, hēnd hōps, hmt.

hōies, homines, hōis. hmōn hujusmodi.

I

Itm ibidem, ipō ipse, incrm̄ incrementum

Imppetu vel imppm̄ imperpetuum.

Ingssuo ingressus, inbcan̄. instantia.

Iur Iurator. Iustic, Iusticiarius.

L

Leb, latitat, legatt or leglio, legalis &c.

libo, libere libtas, littime, legittime.

lra litera, lro, lra, lras, lris.

M

mīa misericordia, & pd doñ in mīa &

mīm minime milline millesimo mr̄ magister

mar or marchle Marescallus, Marcschalsie.

midd, Middlesex, mis, misis &

mañ Manerium hm̄ ppm̄ mēdñum.

N   tertiam partem Manerium

Narr, narracio, Natlis natalis nob nobis

Plate 13.

Words comonly contracted in Old Charters &c, continued.

noster, nostri, nostrum, nostris, nostrorum, nostris.

nomen, nominis, nomine.

nominatur, nuper, nunquam.

O.

omnes, or omnes omnes. omnem, omnt, omnt.

omnium, omnibz. omnio omnio, Omnino.

omnimodum, omittit, omittas &c.

P.

perpetuum pertinentijs &c.

patris parliamentum &c.

patria, patriam. predictis.

preteritus placitum &c

proximus, postea proprius &c

propter. plegij de profequendo.

sno, ponit loco suo. proximus &c.

Q.

Querens, querela,

R.

ad recognoscendum &c.

Plate 14

Words comonly contracted in Old Charters &c continued.

Rospetus, Respectus, Responsū, responsum.

Rectoria, Rectoria, Rñi, Regni, Rotlo, Rotulo,

Rōne, Ratione, Rōnabiliō, Rationabilis &c

§

Sabbti, Sabbathi, Sacramentū, Sacramentum &c

Salutem, Salutem, Vrē (m̄ittre) Sctem &c

Scūs, Scñi Scõr, Sanctus, Sancti Sanctorum

Scūndus, Secundus, Sect, Sectia,

Scaccarium, Scaccarium, Scdm Scco, the Exchequer

Silr, simili, silio silis silit? silic silib3.

Scilt or ss for Scilicet, supdcus, supradictus

Spec or speificabb? specificatus &c

Summ, summonitus, summ fuit ad respondend

Suppoit suppositus Spalis, Specialis. —

Spūalis, spiritualis &c.

§

Tlo, tale, ttlis; ttluo, titulus, tituli.

Tenementū tenementum tenemti tenementi &c

T for Teste in Writs as T Rotto Raymond &c

Plate 15.

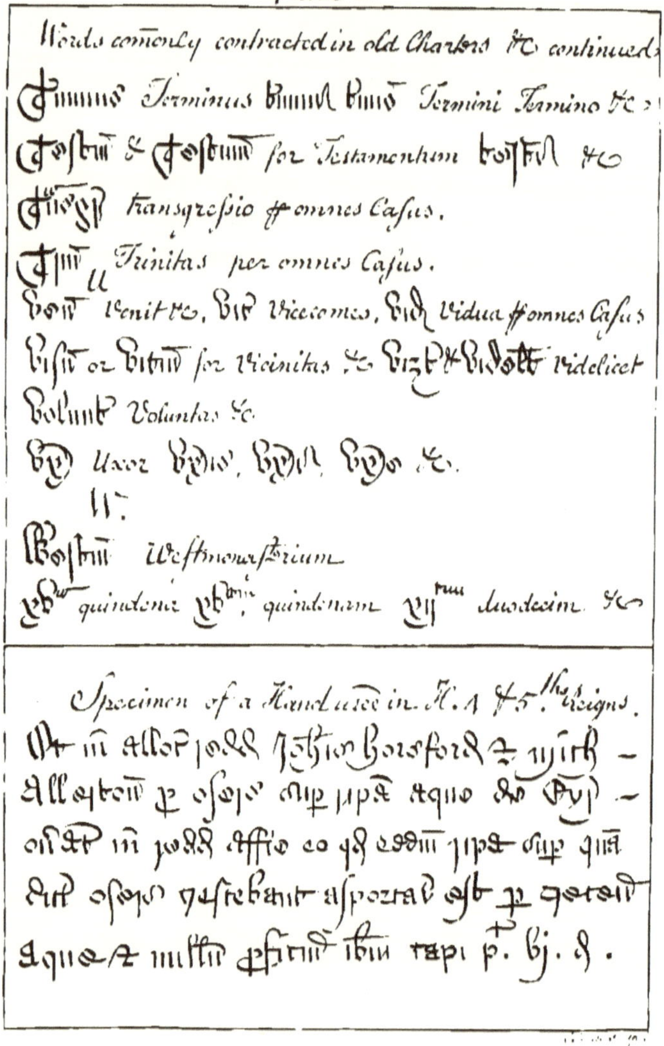

Words comonly contracted in old Charters &c continued.

ꝥ Terminus ꝥ Terminus Termini Termino &c

ꝥ & ꝥ for Testamentum &c

ꝥ transgressio ꝥ omnes Casus.

ꝥ Trinitas per omnes Casus.

Venit &c, Vicecomes, Vidua ꝥ omnes Casus

Vicinitas &c videlicet

Voluntas &c.

Uxor &c.

W.

Westmonasterium

quindena quindenam duodecim &c

Specimen of a Hand used in H. 4 & 5.ᵗʰᵉ Reigns.

(manuscript text in secretary hand, largely illegible)

aqua &c mittit ꝓ ꝑ p. vj. s.

PLATE XV.

Et in Allocatione Redditus Johannis Horsford & Michaelis
Allerton pro osers super ripam Aque de Eyr
oneratis in redditu assise eoquod eadem ripa super quam
dicte osers crescebant asportata est per crecen˙
aque & nullum proficuum ibidem capi potest — Vj".

Hen. IV. & V.

Plate 16.

The Counties of England & Wales will be found thus Written.

Bedford.   Rutland.
Berks, Bucks.   Salop, Sonus, Salop, Somset.
Cambridge.   Stafford.
Chester.   Suffolk.
Cornwall.   Surry.
Derby, Devon.   Sussex.
Dorset.   Southton.
Durham.   Warwick.
Essex.   Westmorland.
York.   Worcester.
Gloucester.   Wilts.
Hereford, Hertford.   **Wales.**
Huntingdon.   Anglesey.
Kent.   Brecock.
Lancaster.   Cardigan.
Leicester.   Carmarthen.
Lincoln.   Carnarvon.
Middlesex.   Denbigh.
Monmouth.   Flint.
Ross, Norfolk.   Glamorgan.
Northampton.   Merioneth.
Northumberland.   Montgomry.
Nottingham.   Pembroke.
Oxford.   Radnor.

Plate 17.

The Bishops of England will be found thus stiled viz.

	Archbishop of Canterbury.
	Winton.
Bishop of	London.
	Lincoln.
	Norwich.
	Salisbury.
	Hereford.
	Worcester.
	Exeter.
	Ely.
	Chichester.
	Rochester.
Epūs	Bath & Wells.
	Coventry & Litchfield
	Glocester.
	Bristol.
	Oxford.
	of the Borough of St. Peter
	al. Peterborow.
	Bangor.
	St. Davids.
	St. Asaph.
	Landaff.
	Archbishop of Yorke.
	Bishop of Durham.
Epūs	Carlisle.
	Chester.

Plate 18.

A general Alphabet of the Old Law Hands.

Plate 19.

The general Alphabet continued.

PLATE XIX.

Robertus Dei gratia Rex Scottorum Omnibus probis hominibus
totius terre sue salutem Sciatis Nos quamdam Cartam
factam per Nos dum eramus Senescallus Scocie Alano Lawedre
fideli nostro de mandato nostro inspectam & diligenter examinatam,
&c.   Anno Regni nostri secundo.

Allerton.   Compotus Rogeri Marschall prepositi ibidem
a festo Sancti Michaelis Anno Regni Regis Henrici Quarti post
Conquestum Sexto usque idem festum Sancti
Michaelis extunc proxime sequentem anno ejusdem Regis
septimo computatum per unum Annum
integrum.

6 & 7 Hen. IV. 2 & 3 Hen. V.

Plate 20.

running Court-hand.

This Indenture made the Eyghte Daye of January,
in the nynth yere of the Reigne of our Sovaigne
Ladye Elizabeth by the grace of god of Englande franure
& Jland Quene Defendo? of the faith &c .

The following Hand much used in 2. Eliz: Reign

This Indenture made sixtenth Day of
November in the Three and fortith yeare of
the raigne of o? sovaigne Ladye Elizabeth
by the grace of god Queene of England &c.

The left Hand formerly used in the Common Pleas.

Come ff. By Anthono Younge gñ nuffo & omo
sitono poffert Augom? Smyth somo Jum̄go
vini mesuagu vini pomeñi? vini Gardinñ
gum̄ ungmi? Aq? tie gum̄ir Aq? p̃t? —
viginta? Aq? paftur? oï London̄ colibẽt? &c.

PLATE XX.

This Indenture made the thirtie daye of Januarye
in the nynth yere of the reigne of our Soveraigne
Ladye Elizabeth by the grace of God of Englande Fraunce
& Ireland Quene Defendor of the Faith, &c.

—————— ——— · ————

This Indenture made thirtenth day of
November in the three and fortith yeare of
the raigne of our Soveraigne Ladye Elizabeth
by the grace of God Queene of England, &c.

— ———————— · ————

Somerset. Scilicet. Precipe Anthonio Yonge quod juste & sine
dilatione reddat Hugoni Smythsonne Armigero
unum mesuagium unum pomarium unum gardinum
quinquaginta acras terre quinque acras prati
viginti acras pasture et undecim solidatas, &c.

PLATE XXX.

Typus Scripturæ in Chartis usitatæ a Temp. Will. Conq. uiq. ad an. 38. Hen. III.
Ex Curûs Thomæ Astleî Arm. R. et Ant. S.S.

Will di gra rex Sciatis me concessisse 7

Temp. W. Conq.

Ego Anselmus see dorobernensis eccte archiep

Temp. W. Rufi

Anno ab incarn dni m. c. xxxiii. facta est hec

A. 33 Hen. I.

Anno ab incarnatione dni cuttt. c. Lii. Gilbert' sippor eccte xpi cant

A. 17. Steph.

Anno ab incarnatoe dni m c Lxxx Anno dict regni H jacf fecunde undecimo fato

A. 22. Hen. II.

Hec est final concordia fca in Curia dni Reg Apd Hornm
facta proximo post exaltacione see crucis Anno etc. Regni Reg Ric.

A. 10. Ric. I.

Hec est final concord fca in cur dni Reg apd noithm Die Lune proximo p fest
sci Bonefch Anno Regni Regis quarto Codm Anno g noiehm cpo Luna Bord

A. 4. Iohis

Dat Londoñ die Lce Luce Euangeliste pontificat nostri Anno Quinto

A. 3. Hen. III.

Anno dni m. cc. L. iiij. In crastino sci Michael Hugo Chumellus abbas de Cremello

A. 38. Hen. III.

PLATE XXI.

Typus Scripturæ in Chartis usitatæ a Temp. Will. Conq. usq. ad annum 38 Hen. III.

Willelmus Dei gratia Rex Sciatis me concessisse, &c.

Temp. W. Conq.

Ego Anselmus Sancte Dorobernensis Ecclesie Archiepiscopus.

Temp. W. Rufi.

Anno ab incarnatione Domini 1133, facta est hec.

Anno 33 Hen. I.

Anno ab incarnatione Domini 1152°, Wibertus Supprior Ecclesie Christi Cantuariensis.

Anno 17 Steph.

Anno ab incarnatione Domini 1175°, Anno autem Regni II. Regis Secundi vicesimo secundo.

Anno 22 Hen. II.

Hec est finalis Concordia facta in Curia Domini Regis apud Notingham
Sabbato proximo post exaltacionem Sancte Crucis Anno decimo Regni Regis Ricardi.

Anno 10 Ric. I.

Hec est finalis concordia facta in Curia Domini Regis apud Notingham die dominica
    proxima post festum
Sancti Botulfi Anno Regni Regis J. quarto coram Domino, J. Norwic. Episcopo Hug. Bard.

Anno 4 Johannis.

Dat' London' die Sancti Luce Evangeliste pontificatus nostri anno quinto.

Anno 5 Hen. III.

Anno Domini 1254°, in crastino Sancti Albani frater Hugo humilis abbas de Tyronnello.

Anno 38 Hen. III.

PLATE XXII.

Typus Scripturae in Chartis usitatae ab A° 56 Hen. III usque ad an° 8 Hen. IV.
Ex Cartis Thomae Astlei Arm. R. et S.S.

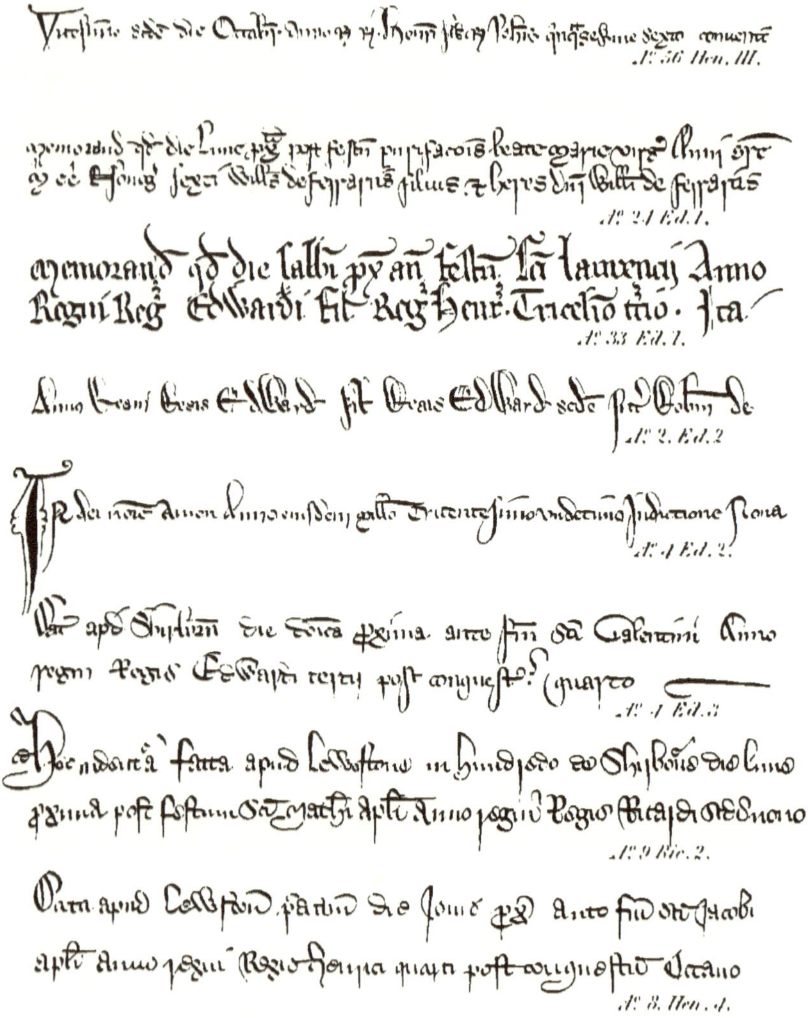
A° 56 Hen. III.
A° 24 Ed. 1.
A° 33 Ed. 1.
A° 2. Ed. 2
A° 4 Ed. 2.
A° 4 Ed. 3
A° 9 Ric. 2.
A° 8. Hen. 4.

PLATE XXII.

Typus Scripturæ in Chartis usitatæ ab Aᵒ 56 Hen. III. usque ad annum 8 Hen. IV.

———— ————

Vicesimo secundo die Octrobris Anno Regni Regis Henrici filij Regis Johannis quinquagesimo sexto convenit.

Anno 56 Hen. III.

Memorandum quod die Lune proxima post festum purificationis beate Marie Virginis Anni Gratie
1296, Willielmus de Ferrarijs filius & heres Domini Willielmi de Ferrarijs.

Anno 24 Edw. I.

Memorandum quod die sabbati proxima ante festum Sancti Laurentij.   Anno
Regni Regis Edwardi filij Regis Henrici tricesimo tertio Ita.

Anno 33 Edw. I.

Anno Regni Regis Edwardi filij Regis Edwardi secundo inter Robertum de.

Anno 2 Edw. II.

In Dei nomine Amen Anno ejusdem Millesimo Tricentesimo Undecimo indictione nona.

Anno 4 Edw. II.

Dat' apud Shirborn die dominica proxima ante festum Sancti Valentini.   Anno
Regni Regis Edwardi tertij post Conquestum quarto.

Anno 4 Edw. III.

Hec Indentura facta apud Lewestone in Hundredo de Shirborne die Lune
proxima post festum Sancti Mathei Apostoli Anno Regni Regis Ricardi Secundi nono.

Anno 9 Ric. II.

Data apud Lewston predictam die Jovis proxima ante festum Sancti Jacobi
Apostoli Anno Regni Regis Henrici Quarti post Conquestum Octavo.

Anno 8 Hen. IV.

PLATE XVIII.

*Typus Scripturæ in Chartis usitatæ ab An̄o 1. Hen. V. usq ad an̄m 30 Eliz. -
Ex Chartis Thomæ Astle A. m. R. et S.S.*

A° 1. Hen. 5.

A° 13. Hen. 6.

A° 13. Ed. 4.

A° 13. Hen. 7.

A° 20. Hen. 8.

A° 2. Ed. 6.

A° 2 & 3 Phil. et Mariæ.

A° 30. Eliz.

PLATE XXIII.

Typus Scripturæ in Chartis usitatæ ab A° 1 Hen. V. usq. ad annum 30 Eliz.

Data apud Sparham die Jovis proxima ante festum Sancti Mathei Apostoli.
Anno Regni Regis Henrici Quinti post Conquestum primo.

Anno 1 Hen. V.

In Witnesse to this present Letteris I have putte to my Seal the 13th day of
Jun, the yere of the Regne of Kyng Henry the Sixte, after the Conquest 15 yeres.

Anno 15 Hen. VI.

In the yere of Oure Lorde Kynge Edwarde the IV^{the}. after the Conqueste of
Ingelonde 13^{the}.

Anno 13 Edw. IV.

Data apud Leweston 14 die Mensis Decembris, Anno Regno Regis
Henrici Septimi quintodecimo.

Anno 15 Hen. VII.

This Indenture made the 12th daye of June, the 20th yere
of the Raygn of Kyng Harry the 8th.

Anno 20 Hen. VIII.

Yoven at Sparham the 16th day of the Moneth of Octobre, in the second
yere of the reigne of Edward the Syxt.

Anno 2 Edw. IV.

Thys Indenture made the tenthe day of Januarie, in the second
and thyrde yere of the reygne of our Sovereygne Lord and Lady Phyllip and Marye.

Anno 2 & 3 Phil. et Marie.

Three and thirteth yere of the reigne of our Soveraigne Ladie
Elizabeth.

Anno 30 Eliz.

D *

AN

APPENDIX.

CONTAINING

THE ANCIENT NAMES OF PLACES

IN

GREAT BRITAIN AND IRELAND,

COLLECTED FROM

ANTONINUS, CÆSAR'S COMMENTARIES, MATTHEW PARIS, LAMBARD, SPELMAN, CAMDEN,
DUGDALE, HECTOR BOETHIUS, BUCHANAN, ARCHBISHOP USHER,
AND OTHER ANCIENT HISTORIANS.

WITH AN

ALPHABETICAL TABLE OF ANCIENT SURNAMES.

*Very necessary for young STUDENTS, and others, who may have Occasion to consult Old
Records, Deeds, Charters; or the Ancient History of Great Britain and Ireland.*

AND

An Exposition of Latin Words,

FOUND IN THE LAW AND OTHER ANCIENT WRITINGS, BUT NOT IN ANY MODERN
DICTIONARY OR GLOSSARY.

F.

APPENDIX.

ANCIENT NAMES OF PLACES.

Note.— *N. B. denotes Places in Scotland, and Ir. in Ireland.*

A.

ABALLABA,
Aballiaba, } *Apulby or Appleby, in Westmorland.*
Applebera, vel
Applebeia,

Abatia,— Abedesberiensis, } *Abotsbury.*

Abbandunum,

Abbendoma, } *Abingdon, in Berkshire, formerly called Sewsham.*
Abendonia,
Abindonia,

Abbas æstuarium, } *The River Humber, in Yorkshire.*
Abum,— Abus,

Abbatia de Berton, *Burton, Staffordshire.*

Aberconovium, } *Aberconway; also the River Conway. See Conovium.*

Aberdona,
Aberdonia, vel } *Aberdeen, in N. B.*
Dœvana,

Aberdlora, } *Aberdore, &* } *in N. B.*
Aberdura, } *Aberdour,*

Abergennium, vel } *Abergavenny, in Monmouthshire.*
Gobannium,

Ablato Bulgio, } *Bulnesse or Bolness, in Cumberland.*

Abona, *The River Avon.*

Abone, } *Avington or Aventon, in Gloucestershire.*
Abonis,

Aboya, *Achboy, in Ireland.*

Abronethæum, *Abernethy, in N. B.*

Abrevicum, *Berwick-upon-Tweed.*

Achadia, *Auvagdoune, in Ireland.*

Achelanda, *Bishops-Auckland, Durham.*

Achilia, *Achill Isles, in Ireland.*

Adelingia, *Athelney, in Somersetshire.*

Ad-Ansam, vel } *Ithanchester, and Coggeshall, in Essex; also Wratting, Suffolk.*
Othona,

Ad-Lapidem, *Stoneham, in Hampshire.*

Ad-Latus, or Bovium, *Boverton, Glamorganshire.*

Ad-Murum, *Waltown.*

Ad-Pontem, } *Paunton, Linc.; also Bridgeford and Southwell, Nott.*

Ad-Tisam, *Piersbridge, Durham.*

Ad-Portum Dubris, *Dover. See Doris.*

Ad-Portum Rutupas, *See Rhitubi Portus.*

Ad-Tuam, *Tasburgh, in Norfolk.*

Adros, vel Andros, } *Bardsey Island, betwixt Wales and Ireland.*
Andrium Edri,

Adurni Portus, *Ederington, in Suffolk.*

Æbudæ, } *The Hebrides, West of Scotland.*

Sancti Ægidii ad Portam Membris Captorum, } *St. Giles, Cripplegate.*

Ælia Castra, *Alchester, Oxfordshire.*

Æliani Porta, } *Anold Town near Hadrian's Wall, in N. B.*

Æsycha, *Netherby, Cumberland.*

Ætona, vel Ætonia, } *Eton, in Buckinghamshire, near Windsor.*

Afena, } *Littleborough.*

Agelocum, } *See Segelocum.*

Agamerium, *Aghamere, in Ireland.*

Ager Maridunensis, *Caermarthenshire.*

Agmundishamum, } *Agmundisham, or Amersham, in Buckinghamshire.*

Agneda, *Edinburgh.*

Akeburgh, *Melsonby, Yorkshire.*

Albana, *Scotland. See Caledonia.*

Alana, *Alloway, in N. B.*

Alannius, *The River Avon, Wilts.*

Alauna— Alnevicum, *Alnwick.*

Alaunicus Portus, *Milford Haven.*

Alaunicus Pons,
Alaunodunum, } *Maidenhead, in Berkshire; called in the Court Rolls of the Manor of Bray, Maidenhuthe, or Maidenhithe.*

Alaunus Flu. vel } *The River Alne, in Northumberland.*
Alanus,

Albion, Alvion,
Pridania, Britannia,
Pritanniæ, Brithania, } *Great Britain.*
Brutania, Pritania,

Sancti Albani in Vico } *St. Alban's, Wood-street, London.*
Ligneo,

Album

Album Monasterium,	*Whitchurch, in Shropshire.*
Alata Castra,	
Alatum Castrum,	
Castrum Puellarum,	*Edinburgh, and Edinburgh*
Edenburgus,	*Castle.*
Edenburgum,	
Dunedinum, vel	
L'Isle,	
Alectem,—Alectum,	
Deidonum,	*Dundee, in N. B.*
Taodunum,	
Alenus Flu.	*The River Allen in Dorset- shire ; another in Den- bighshire ; also the River Alne in Warwickshire.*
Alexodunum,	*Brough on the Sands, Cum- berland.*
Alecana,	*Ichly, Yorkshire.*
Alion,—Alione,	*Lancaster; also Whitlaw*
Alone,	*Castle, in Cumberland.*
Alone Flu.	*The River Alne, in North- umberland.*
Alpes Peneni Montes,	*Pendle Hill, Lancashire.*
De Alto Pecco,	*The Castle in the Peak, Derbyshire.*
Alunna,	*Castleshaw, Yorkshire.*
Amboglanua, vel	*Ambleside, in Westmor- land.*
Ambegianna,	
Ambrosia,	
Ambrosii Burgus,	*Amesbury, in Wilts.*
Ambrosii Mons,	
Amenissima,	*Gogmagog Hills, near Cambridge.*
Montana de Balsham,	
Ancalites,	*The Hundred of Henley, in Oxfordshire.*
Anderida,	*Newenden upon the Rother, in Kent.*
Noviodunum,	
Andevera,	*Andover, in Hampshire.*
Andovera,	
Andreapolis.	*See Fanum Reguli.*
Andreæ sub Malo cereali,	*St. Andrew's, Under- shaft,*
Andreæ ad Vestinrium,	*St. Andrew's, Ward- robe,*
Annæ intra Portam Alucani,	*St. Ann's, Aldersgate,*
Annæ nigrorum Monachorum,	*St. Ann's, Blackfriars,*
Anglesega, or Mona,	*Anglesey.*
Anguillaria Insula,	*The Isle of Ely.*
Anguillarianum Monasterium,	*The City of Ely.*
Heliense Cœnobium,	

Angelocum,	*Ancaster, Lincolnshire.*
Æliensis, or Eliensis,	*Of Ely.*
Angusia,	*Angus, in N. B.*
Ansoba, Ansoba,	*Galway Bay, also Lough Corbes, Ireland.*
Antivestæum,	*The Land's End.*
Apiacum,	*Pap Castle, in Cumberland.*
Aqua Rubra,	*Redburn. See Durovo- brivæ.*
Aquæ Calidæ,	
Aquis Solis,	
Akemancester,	*City of Bath, in Somerset- shire.*
Badiza,—Balnea,	
Batha,—Bathonia,	
Aquædon,	*Eidure, or Eaton.*
Aquædunum,	
Aquædunensis Saltus,	*Waterden, Norfolk.*
Aquævadensis Pons,	*Elford.*
Aquilædunum,	*Hoxten, or Eglestone.*
Arbeia,	*Ireby, in Cumberland.*
Archelandria,	*Auckland, in Durham.*
Arclovium,	*Arklow,*
Ardræum,	*Ardee, — in Ireland.*
Ardraicum,	
Argadia,	*Ardagh,*
Argathelia,	*The Hill of Gathel, now*
Ardgathel, vel	*called Argyll, in N. B.*
Earraghaoidheal,	
Argita,	*Swilley Lake, in Ireland.*
Ariconium,	*Kenchester, near Hereford ; also Cirencester.*
Armacha,	*Ardmagh, or Armagh, in Ireland.*
Ardmacha,	
Magh-ard,	
Armanothia,	*Ardmeanach, in N. B.*
Arundelia,	*Arundel, in Sussex.*
Arnudellum,	
Aruntina Vallis,	*Redbridge, in Hampshire.*
Arundinis Vadum,	
Arunus Flu.	*The River Aron, in Sussex.*
Arvonica,	*Caernarvonshire.*
Arus Flu.	*The River Are, in York- shire.*
Asaphensis Episcopa- tus,	*The Bishoprick of St. Asaph.*
Athanaton,	*Isle of Thanet.*
Athanatos,	*See Tanathos.*
Athesis Flu.	*The River Tees. See Tesa.*
Atholia,	*Athol, in N. B.*
Athra,	*Athenry, in Ireland.*
Attrebati,	*People of Berkshire.*
Aula, vel Villa Antiqua,	*Aldbury, Herts.*

Aurea

Aurea Vallis, *Golden Vale, in Hertford-shire.*

Ausona, vel
Antona, vel
Antona, vel *The River Nine, or Nen, in Northamptonshire.*
Aufona,

Avalonia, *Glastonbury, in Somerset-shire.*

Ave, Avinus, *River Avon, or Avin, in N.D.*

Angusta, *London.*
Trinobantum, See Londinense oppidum.

Anterii, *People of Atterith, Atheury, or Athy, in Ireland.*

Avona Flu. *Avon, in Wiltshire.*
The River Avon, that runs by Malmesbury, Brad-ford, Bath, Bristol.
The River Nen, that runs through Northampton, by Oundle, Peterborough, and into the Sea near Lynn.
The Avon, that flows by Amesbury, Salisbury, and so into Dorsetshire.

Avona Flu. *The Waveney, that divides Norfolk and Suffolk, runs by Bungay, corruptly so called for Avoney.*
The Avon, rising not far from Naseby, in North-amptonshire, runs by Warwick, Stratford, Eve-sham, and into the Severn, at Tewkesbury.

Avona, *Bungay, in Suffolk.*

Avona,
Avondunum, *Hampton Court, according to Leland, also South-ampton.*

Avonæ Vallis, *Avondule, or Oundle, in Northamptonshire.*

Avonii palatium, *Winchester House, South-wark.*

Axelodunum, *Hexam, in the Bishoprick of Durham.*
Hangustaldensis, *Of Hexam.*

B.

BACHELAGANÆ
Sylvæ,
Bagiloganæ, *Bagley.*

Badiza,
Balnea,
Batha,
Bathonia, *City of Bath. See Aquæ Calidæ.*

Badonicus Mons, *Bannes-down, a Hill over a little Village near Bath, called Bathstone.*

Bainardi Castellnm, *Baynard's Castle, London.*
Bainus Pons, *Bainbridge, in Yorkshire.*

Banatia, *Bausey or Bean Castle, in N.D.*

Bannavenna,
Bannaventa,
Bennaventa, *Northampton. See Northantonia & Isan-navantia.*

Banus Flu. *The River Ban, in Lincoln-shire.*

Bana Insula, *An Island, about three miles from the River Tuff, in Glamorganshire.*

Bardunus, *A River near Norwich, in Norfolk.*

Sancti Bartholomæi pone Peristylium, *St. Bartholomew, near the Exchange, London.*

Barvicus,
Barwicus,
Berwicus,
Borcovium,
Borcovins,
Borcovicus, *Berwick-upon-Tweed. See Abrevicum.*

Basenga,
Basingnm,
Basingum, *Basing, in Hampshire.*

Batersega, *Battersey, in Surrey.*

Batilfordia,
Dunum Manapia, *Waterford, in Ireland.*

Bebba, *Bamborough.*

Bedfordia,
Bedefordia,
Budeforda, *Bedford.*

Belgæ Somerseti, *The Inhabitants of Somer-set, Wilts, & Hampshire.*

Belerium prom. vel
Bolerium prom. *The Land's End. See Antivestænm.*

Bellinus Sinus, *Billingsgate.*

Belisama, *Ribble River, or Rhibel-mouth, in Lancashire.*

Bellelanda, *Byland, in Yorkshire.*

Bello-clivum,
Bello-desertum,
Bellus Locus, *Beldesert, or Beaudesert, in Warwickshire.*

Bello situm, vel
Isidis vadum, *City of Oxford. See Oxenforda.*

Sanctus Benedictus in Graminoso Vico, *St. Bennet, Grace-church-street, London.*

Bennores

Bennones, vel
Vennones, } *Claybrook, in Leicestershire.*
Bearrokscira,
Berocia,
Berkeria, } *Berkshire.*
Bercheria,
Berchensis, } *Of, or belonging to Berk-*
Beruchensis, } *shire.*
Berechingum, *Barking, in Essex.*
Berelea, } *Berkley, in Gloucestershire.*
Berchelcia,
Berigonium, { *Bargenny, in N. B. and a*
{ *Creek there.*
Bermundi Insula, *Bermondsey, in Surrey.*
Bernardi Castellum, { *Bernard Castle, in the Bi-*
{ *shoprick of Durham.*
Bernicia, { *Was a Province reaching*
{ *from the River Tees to*
{ *Edinburgh Frith, in N.B.*
Beverlea, *Beverley, in Yorkshire.*
Beverlacensis, { *Of, or belonging to Bever-*
{ *ley.*
Berubium, { *Urdhead, a Promontory in*
{ *N. B.*
Bibrocassi, { *The Hundred of Bray, in*
Bibroci, { *Yorkshire.*
Bimonium Vinocium,
Brinonium Vinovia,
Binonium, } *Binchester, in the Bishop-*
Binovia, } *rick of Durham.*
Binovium,
Bishamum, } *Bustleham, or Bisham, in*
Bustelli Domus, } *Berkshire.*
Blacamora, { *Blackmore, part of the*
{ *North Riding of York-*
{ *shire.*
Bladinæ Montes, { *Mountains of Ossory, in*
{ *Ireland.*
Bladunum, See *Maidulphi Curia.*
Blaneafurda, *Blundford, in Dorsetshire.*
Blancum Castrum, { *Blane Castle, in Monmouth-*
{ *shire.*
Blatum Bulginm, *Tynemouth; also Boulness,*
Ablato Bulgio, *in Cumberland.*
Blestium, { *Gloucester; also Old Town,*
{ *in Herefordshire.*
Boanda, { *The River Boyne, in Ir.*
Boandus, { *made remarkable by King*
Burindus, { *William's crossing it, and*
{ *defeating the forces of*
{ *James II.*
Boccinum, } *Buckingham, and Bucken-*
Buckinghamia, } *ham.*

Buckingensis, *Of Buckingham.*
Bodiamum, *Bodiam, in Sussex.*
Bodotria, *Edinburgh Frith.*
Boduni, See Dobuni.
Boghania, vel } *Buchanan, or*
Buchania, } *Buquehain, in N. B.*
Bonium, seu { *Boverton, or Cowbridge,*
Bovium, { *in Glamorganshire; also*
{ *Bangor, or Banchor, in*
{ *Flintshire.*
Borreum prom. *St. Ellen's Cape.*
Bosphorus Picticus, *Pentland Frith, in N. B.*
Botelega, *Boulney, near Oxford.*
Sancti Botolphi Alneæ } *St. Botolph, Alders-*
portæ, *gate,*
Saucti Botolphi ad } *St. Botolph, Billings-*
portam Bellini, *gate,*
Sancti Botolphi ad } *St. Botolph, Aldgate,*
Veterem portam,
Sancti Botolphi ad } *St. Botolph, Bishops-*
Episcopi portam, } *gate,* } *London.*
Boxleia, *Boxley, in Kent.*
Brabonincum,
Brocavo,
Brocavum, { *Brougham, in Westmorland,*
Broconiacum, { *also Bewcastle and Car-*
Brovonacis, { *lisle, in Cumberland.*
Brovonacum,
Bracchium, *Burgh, in Yorkshire.*
Brachilega, { *Brackley, in Northampton-*
{ *shire.*
Bramptonia, { *Brampton, near Hunting-*
{ *don.*
Brannodunum Portus, *Brancaster, in Norfolk.*
Braunogenium,
Branovium,
Branoricum, } *The City of Worcester.*
Branconium,
Brannovium,
Bravinium,
Brechinia, *Brecknock.*
Bremenium, } *Rochester, in Northumber-*
Bramenium, } *land.*
Brementonacum, *Overborough and Lancaster.*
Brementaracum, *Brampton, in Cumberland.*
Brentæ Vadus, *Brentford, in Middlesex.*
Brigantes, { *Inhabitants of Yorkshire,*
Brigæ, { *Lancashire, Bishoprick of*
{ *Durham, Westmorland,*
{ *and Cumberland; also of*
{ *Waterford and Kilkenny,*
{ *in Ireland.*
Brigantium, *York.* See Eboracum.
Brige

Brige, vel
Brage,
Brigus, vel
Birgus, } *Broughton, in Hampshire.*

} *Barrow River, in Ireland.*

Bristolia,
Bristolium,
Bristowa, } *The City of Bristol.*

Bristoliensis, vel
Bristowensis, } *Of Bristol, or Bristow.*

Britanni,
Britones, } *People of Britain.*

Britannicus Portus,
Callisia, Iecius portus, } *Calais, in France.*

Britanodunum, *Dumbarton, in N. B.*
Bromfelda, *Bromfeld, in Denbighshire.*
Bucostenum, *Buxton, in Derbyshire.*
Bullæum Silurum, *Buelth, in Brecknockshire.*
Burrium, { *Uske, in Monm.; also Dow-*
{ *ard, Heref.*

C.

CACARIA, vel
Calcaria, } *Tadcaster, Aberford, or Hel-*
caster, in Yorkshire.

Calatam,
Caermardinia,
Carmarthinia, } *Caermarthen, in Wales.*

Caerperis, *Portchester.*
Caerseverus, *See Mons Arenosns.*
Caer Lincoit, *Lincoln. See Lincolnia.*
Cæsaria, *Jersey Isle.*
Cæsaro-uangus, { *Braughin, Herts. Burgsted,*
{ *Brentwood, in Essex.*
Calncum,
Calagum, } { *Overborough, in Lancash.;*
{ *also Whelp Castle, in*
{ *Cumberland.*

Calabrinm Nemus, { *The Forest of Galtrees, in*
{ *Yorkshire.*
Calderus Flu. { *The River Calder, in York-*
{ *shire.*
Caledonia, *Scotland.*
Caledonius Oceanus, *The Scottish Sea.*
Caledonii, { *Those that inhabited both*
{ *sides of the Grampian*
{ *Mountains in N. B.*
Calleva Attrebatum, *Farnham, Surrey.*
Caleva, vel
Calena, } *See Gallena.*

Calna, *Calne, in Wiltshire.*
Calonia, *Coldingham.*
Camaletum, *Camalet Castle.*
Camalodunum,
Camoladunum,
Camolodunum,
Camoludunum, } *Maldon, in Essex, accord-*
Camudolanum, *ing to Camden; but, accord-*
Camulodunum, *ing to others, Colchester.*
Mealdunum, vel
Colonia Victricensis, }
Cambium Regale,
Bursa, } *The Royal Exchange, Lon-*
Excambium Regium, *don.*
Peristylium,
Cambodunum, { *Almondbury, or the Ruins*
Campordunum, { *near Almonbury, in York-*
Camulodunum, { *shire.*
Camboricum, *Granchester.*
Camboritum,
Camboricum,
Cantabrigia, } *Cambridge, and Hogmagoy,*
in Cambridgeshire.
Cambretonium,
Cambretovinm, } *Breton Spring, or a Place*
near it, in Suffolk.
Comvetronum,
Cambria, *Wales. See Wallia.*
Campus Altus, { *Hatfield, or Hautfield, in*
{ *Hertfordshire.*
Campus Novo Forensis, *Newmarket-Heath.*
Candalia, } *Kendal, and Kendal Barony,*
Concangium, } *in Westmorland.*
Candida Casa, *Whitcherne, in N. B.*
Canganum,
Cauganorum, } *See Ganganorum.*

Canonium, { *Canonden, Chelmsford,*
{ *Chensford, or Chenford,*
{ *and Ring-Hill, in Es-*
{ *sex.*
Cantuaritæ, *Kentish Saxons.*
Cantia,
Cantium, } *Kent.*
Cantium promonto-
rium, } *The North Foreland.*
Cantæ, *The People of Ross, in N.B.*
Cantuaria, *Canterbury City.*
Cantuarensis, *Of Canterbury.*
Capræ Caput, *See Gabrosentum.*
Carboriarius Collis, *Coleshill, in Flintshire.*
Carcaria, *Aberford.*
Carricta, *Carrick, in N. B.*
Carleolum, *Curlisle. See Lucopibia.*
Cardigania, *Cardigan,* }
Carnarvonia, *Caernarvon,* } *in Wales.*
Carenii,

Carenii, { Inhabitants of Cathensis, in N. B., according to Camden. Ortelius places them more Northward than the Carnonacæ on the West Side of N. B.

Carnonacæ, Canovaci, { The People of Lenox, or those who inhabited beyond the River Longas, on the West Side of N.B.

Curphillis, { A famous Castle, supposed to have been built by the Romans, in Glamorganshire.

Cassi, Cassii, } The Hundred of Cashio, in Hertfordshire.

Cassilensis, Of Cashel, in Ireland.
Cassiterides, The Islands of Scilly.
Cassivelaunnioppidum, St.Alban's.SeeVerolamium
Castra Alata, See Alata Castra, &c.
Castra exploratorum, { Burgh on the Sands, in Cumberland.
Castrum de Vies, Divisæ, } The Devizes, in Wiltshire.
Castrodunum,
Castrum Oscæ, Uske. See Burrium.
Contaracta Flu. vel Cataracta, } The River Swale, in Richmondshire.
Cataracta, Cataractonium, Cataractnarium, } Catterick Bridge, and Merton, in Yorkshire.
Cataractorum, Alerton, in Yorkshire.
Catini, { The People of Caithness, in N. B.
Cattidudani, Cattitudani, Catticuclani, Cathieludani, Cathrieludani, Cattnellani, Cattieuchlani, } The People of Buckingham, Bedford, and Hertfordshire.
Cathania, Caithness, in N. B.
Caverna Viperina, { Assenden, or Aspenden, in Hertfordshire.
Cauci, Chauci, Eblani, Iberi, Iverni, Simeni, Uterni, } The People of Ireland.
Cerda, Selgovarum, } Dumfries, in N. B.

Cestria, Chestria, Chestrum, } Chester City, or West-Chester.
Cirencestria, Corinium, } Circester, or Cirencester, in Gloucestershire.
Clara, vel Claria, County of Clare, in Ireland.
Cavoda, Cawood, in Yorkshire.
Canna, See Convenos.
Causennæ, Causennis, } Brough Hill, Lincolnshire. See Gausennæ.
Cavum Deiram, Cavæ Diræ, } Holderness, in Yorkshire.
Ceangi & Cangi, { People about Cheshire, according to Camden.
Celnius, { Supposed to be the River Keillan; it rises below Mount Grampus in N.B. and falls into the German Ocean.
Ceninaghi, See Iceni.
Cenion } Flu. Como } { The River by Tregony, in Cornwall.
Centum fontes, Hundreds-kelde.
Cerdici vadum, Chardford, in Hampshire.
Ceretica, Ceretici, } Cardiganshire.
Cernelicnse cœnobium, Cerne, in Dorsetshire.
Cerones, Cerouii, { The Inhabitants of Assinshire, in N. B., according to Camden.
Ceroti Insula, Certosia, Cervi Insula, } Chertsey, in Surrey; or Hartlepool, in the Bishoprick of Durham.
Chineglishi Castrum, Kenilworth Castle.
Cheva, Kew, in Surrey.
Chirca, Chirk, in Denbighshire.
Ciceastria, Cicestria, } Chichester, in Sussex.
Cilurinum, Cilurnum, } Callerton, or Collerford, in Northumberland.
Clamoventa, Clanoventa, } See Glannibanta.
Clara-fontanus, Clarus fons, } Sherborne, in Dorsetshire.
Claudia, Claudiocestria, } Gloucester.
Clevum, vel Glevum, } See Glavorna.
Clausentum, Hamptuna, Southamptonia, Trisanton, Trisontonis portus, } Southampton Town, in Hampshire.
Cluanania, Clonmel, in Ireland.
Clonensis

Clonensis Episcopatus	The Bishoprick of Clonmel.
Cluida,	The River Clwyd, in Denbighshire.
Coccinm, vel Goccium,	Ribchester, in Lancashire.
Cocarus, Cokarus,	The River Coke, in Yorkshire; and Cocar, in Lancashire.
Colonia, Coludi, Coldania, Colcestria, Colonia, Coluum Pontes.	Collington, in N. B. Haverhill, Colchester, Colne, or Sudbury, in Essex. Colnbrook, or Colebrook, in Middlesex, and Bucks.
Combretoninm,	Icklingham, Suffolk.
Conacta, Connatehtia,	The Province of Connaught, in Ireland. Tirconnell, in Ireland.
Conallea, Connaria, Conneria,	Connor, in Ireland.
Concangium, Coneani, Condate, Comlercum,	The Barony of Kendal. The People of Munster in Ir. Congleton, in Cheshire. Chester upon the Street, in the Bishoprick of Durham.
Cæsaro-Magus. Canonium, Canovium.	Chelmsford, in Essex. Caerhead upon Conway, in Caernarvonshire.
Conorium, Conovius, vel Novius,	The River Conway, that divides Caernarvonshire from Denbighshire; also the Town of Conway or Aberconway.
Convennon, Convennos Insula. Connos,	Convey, or Sheppey Island, at the mouth of the River Thames.
Conventria, Coventria,	Coventry City, in Warwickshire.
Coqueda Insula.	The Isle of Coquet, on the Coast of Northumberland.
Coqueda, Coquedus,	Coquet River, in Northumberland.
Corcagia, Corragia,	The City of Cork.
Coria, vel Corta Damniorum, Coria,	Camelon, in N. B.
Corstopilti. Corstopilum. Corstopitum. Caria, Curia Ottadinorum,	Corbridge, or Curebridge, upon Tyne; also Morpeth and Gembletpeth, in Northumberland.
Corinea, Cornubia, Cornwallia, Occidua Wallia,	Cornwall.
Corinium,	Cirencester, in Gloucestershire, according to Camden.
Corinus Flu.	The River Churne, that runs by Cirencester.
Coritani, vel Coritavi,	People of Northampton, Leicester, Rutland, Derby, and Nottingham shires.
Cornavii, vel Cornabii,	Inhabitants of Warwick, Worcester, Stafford, Shropshire, & Cheshire.
Cornabii, Corabui, Logi,	The People of Strathnavern, in N. B.
Cornutum Monasterium,	Hornchurch, in Essex.
Cotteswoldia,	Cotswold, in Gloucestershire.
Covi Berchilega, vel Burchelega,	Coverley, in Gloucestershire.
Cranburna, Craneburgum, Burginatium,	Cranborne, in Dorsetshire: or Conenburgh, in Cleveland.
Cravena,	Craven, in Yorkshire.
Crecolada, vel Græcolada,	Cricklade, or Creeklade, in Wiltshire.
Cridea,	Crediton, or Kirton, in Devonshire.
Crococalana, Crocolana,	Ancaster, in Lincolnshire.
Crowlandia, Croylandia, Crulandia, Crulandensis,	Crowland, in Lincolnshire. Of Crowland.
Crux Chariniana,	Charing Cross.
Cumbria, Cumberlandia,	Cumberland.
Cumbri,	The People of Cumberland.
Cunetio,	Edgbury, in Hampshire; and Marlborough, in Wiltshire.
Curia Edmundi, Burgus,	Bury St. Edmund's. See Villa Faustini.

D.

DACORUM CLADES,	Danes-end, in Hertfordshire.
Dabrona,	The River Avennon, in Ireland.

Damnii,

Damnii, { *The People of Clydesdale, and of Westmorland.*

Damnonii,
Dannonii,
Dumnonii,
Dunmonii, } *The People of Devonshire and Cornwall.*

Dommnceusis,
Domnonicusis, } *Of Devonshire.*

Danica Sylva,
Danubiæ, } { *Andredswald Forest, in Sussex; also the Forest of Dean, in Gloucester-shire.*

Danmoniorum regio,
Devonia,
Dommonia,
Domnonia, } *Devonshire.*

Danmoniorum pro-montorium, } *The Lizard Point, in Corn-wall.*

Danum, { *Doncaster, in Yorkshire, & Littleborough, in Nott.*

Danus Flu. { *The Dane, in Lincolnshire; the Dan, or Daven, in Cheshire; the Don, or Dun, in Yorkshire.*

Darbia, vel
Derbia,
Darbiensis, } *The Town of Derby.*

Comitatus Dorven-tania, } *Derbyshire.*

Darentus Flu.
Dorventa, } *Darent, or Dart River, in Kent.*

Darrentia, { *The River Derwent, in Der-byshire.*

Darotenses,
Durotriges, } *People of Dorsetshire.*

Darvernorum,
Darvernum,
Dorobrevum,
Durobrevis,
Durobrevum,
Durobrius,
Durobrovæ,
Duropronis,
Duroprovis,
Hrosi, vel
Rhesi Civitas,
Rofia, Roibis,
Roffi Civitas, } *The City of Rochester, in Kent.*

Darvernum,
Dorbernia,
Dorobellum,
Durovernum,
Durorvernum, } *Canterbury. See Cantuaria.*

Deiloenm,

Deira, } { *The part of the Kingdom of the Northumbrians on the South Side of the Tyne.*

Deirorum Sylva, } { *Deer-wald, or Beverley, in Yorkshire.*

Deira Sylva, } { *Deerhurst, in Gloucester-shire.*

Dela, *Deal, in Kent.*
Delgovitia, *Godmanham, in Yorkshire.*
Delvinia, } { *Delvin, in Westmeath, Ire-land.*

Demetæ,
Dimetæ,
Demetia, } *People of West Wales.*

Denbighia, *West Wales.*
Dercutivadum, *Denbigh, in Denbighshire.*
Dartford, in Kent.

Derventio,
Derwentio,
Dorovcntio,
Dorventa, } { *Auldby upon Derwent, in Yorkshire; also Darwent River in Yorkshire, Der-byshire, and Cumber-land.*

Dera Flu. *The River Dee, in Cheshire.*
Deva, *Chester, or Dundee.*
Devana Urbs,
Deunana,
Duinana, } *Chester. See Cestria.*
Legio XX Victrix, }

Dasmonia, *Desmond, in Ireland.*
Dictum, } { *Diganway, in Caernarvon-shire.*

Divilina,
Dublinia,
Dubliuium,
Eblana, } { *Divilin, Double-Inn, now called Dublin, the capital City of Ireland.*

Divisæ,
Divisio,
Dobuni,
Dotuni, } { *The Derizes, in Wiltshire. See Castrum de Vies. The People of Gloucester-shire and Oxfordshire.*

Dorfris,
Dubris,
Doris, } *Dover, in Kent.*

Dorcestria,
Dorkcestria,
Dorkcestria,
Dornsetta,
Dunium,
Durnium, } { *Dorchester and Wareham, in Dorsetshire.*

Durnovaria, vel
Duruonovaria,
Dorsetania,
Dorsetia,
Dura Provincia, } *Dorsetshire.*

Godstow, in Oxfordshire.

Dorciuia,

Dorcinia, vel
Dorcinii Civitas,
Durocastrum,
Hydropolis,
} *Dorchester, in Oxfordshire.*

Doris Cantiorum,
Dorobrina,
Dovoria,
Dovorria,
Doveria,
Duris,
} *Dover. See Dorfris.*

Dorobernia,
Doroveruum,
Durovernum,
} *Canterbury. See* Cantuaria.

Dorpendnnum. *Orpington, in Kent.*
Dorus Flu. *The Dor, in Hertfordshire.*
Dovus Flu. *The Dove, in Derbyshire.*
Ducalidonii, *The Scots. See* Scoti.
Dumna, *Fair Island.*
Dunelmensis Comita-} *The County of the Bishop-*
tus, *rick of Durham.*

Dunelmia,
Dunelmum.
Dunelmus,
Dunholmus.
Dunholmum,
} *Durham City.*

Dunum, vel
Dunus Sinus,
} *The Creek at Dunsbey, near Whitby, in Yorkshire.*

Dunvicus,
Dunwicus, alias
Felicis oppidum,
} *Dunmock, alias Flixton, in Suffolk.*

Dunam,
Duri,
Duris,
Down.
The River Dur, } *in Ireland.*

Durobrevis,
} *An old Town, called Dor-manchester, on the River Nen, in Northampton-shire.*

Durobrivæ,
} *Dornford and Caster, in Huntingdonshire, and Tattershall, in Lincoln-shire,*

Durocobrivæ, vel
Aqua Rubra,
} *Ravensborough Castle, and Redburn, in Hertford-shire.*

Durocornovium, vel
Passorum Urbs,
} *Cirencester; also Dorchest. See Cirencestria.*

Durolenum,
Durolerum,
} *Newington, or Lenham and Ashford, in Kent.*

Durolipons,
Durosipons.
} *Godmanchester and Ches-terton, in Huntingdon-shire.*

Durolitum,
} *Layton, or Old Ford, in Es-sex; and Cheshunt, Herts.*

E.

EAST-SEXENA,
Essexia,
Est-Sexa,
} *Essex.*

Ebodia, *The Isle of Alderney.*
Eboracum,
Eburacum,
} *York City.*

Eboracensis Ager, vel
Comitatus,
} *Of the County of York.*

Ebudæ,
Incades,
Hebrides,
Lucades,
} *Western Isles of N.B.*

Ebuda, vel
Hebuda secunda,
Hebuda occidentalior
Levissa,
} *Lewis Island, the largest of the Hebrides.*

Saucti Edmundi in } *St. Edmund, in Lombard*
Vico Longobardico,} *Street.*
Edmundi Burgus, *St.Edmondsbury,in Suffolk.*
Eilecuriani Vallis, } *The Vale of Aylesbury, in*
Eilecurium. } *Buckinghamshire.*
Eilimenou Gabranto-} *Sowerby, or Everley, in*
nicorum, } *Yorkshire.*
Eimotus Flu. { *The River Eimot, in Cumberland.*

Elgotii,
Elgoræ,
Selgoræ,
} *Inhabitants of Liddisdale, Eusdale, Eskdale, and Annandale, in Scotland.*

Eliensis Insula, *The Isle of Ely.*
Ellandunum, { *The old Name of Wilton, in Wiltshire.*
Elteshamum, *Eltham, in Kent.*
Eminentior extensio } *Eatonness, in Suffolk.*
prom.
Emonia, *MaidIsle,ontheEastofN.B.*
Eovesum,
Evestamum,
} *Evesham, or Evesholme, in Worcestershire.*

Epeiacum, vel
Epiacum,
} *See Apiacum.*

Etocetum,
{ *Barbeacon, in Staffordshire: or according to Camden, Uttoxeter.*

Epidinm,
Epidiorum,
{ *The Mull of Cantyre, in N.B. The Island that is near Cantyre is likewise called Epidium.*

Erdini, *People of Fermanagh, in Ir.*
Ernulphi Curia, { *Einsbury in St. Neot's, Huntingdonshire.*
Eubonia, *Isle of Man. See* Mannia.
Evenlodns Flu. { *The River Evenlode, in Oxfordshire.*

Evonium.

Evonium,	*Dunstaffnage, in N. B.*
Excambium Regium,	*See* Cambium Regale.
Exa Flu. Isaca, Isca,	*The River Ex, in Devonshire.*
Exonia, Isca, Isca Danmoniorum vel Dunmoniorum, Isca & Scudum Nunniorum,	*Exeter City, in Devonshire.*

F.

FALA Flu.	*The River Vale, in Cornwall.*
Falensis portus, Voluba,	*Falmouth, in Cornwall.*
Fanum Sancti Albani, Villa Albani,	*St. Alban's, in Hertfordish.*
FanumSanctiJohannis,	*St. John's Town, in Ireland.*
Fanum Iltuti,	*St. Llantwit, in Glamorganshire.*
Fanum Ivonis Persiæ,	*St. Ive's, in Huntingdonshire.*
Fanum Leonis,	*Leominster. See* Leonense Cœnobium.
Fanum Neoti,	*St. Neot's, in Huntingdonshire.*
Fanum Reguli,	*St. Andrew's, in N. B.*
Fauum Sancti Stephani,	*Kirkby-Stephen, in Westmorland.*
Faustini Villa,	*St.Edmundsbury,in Suffolk.*
Fawenses,	*Inhabitants of Fowey, in Cornwall.*
Fibrilega, Fibrolega,	*Beverley, Yorkshire.* *See* Beverlea.
Fisburgingi,	*A People in or near Northumberland.*
Flintia,	*Flint Town.*
Flintensis Comitatus,	*Flintshire.*
Fons Amnensis,	*Amwell, in Hertfordshire.*
Fons Brigidæ,	*Bridewell, in London.*
Fons clarus,	*Sherborne, in Dorsetshire.*
Fons interfraxinus,	*Ashwell, in Hertfordshire.*
Fontanensis Ecclesia,	*Wells, in Somersetshire.*
Fretum Britannicum, Fretum Gallicum, Fretum Morinorum,	*The Streights of Calais.*
Fromus Flu.	*The River Frome, in Gloucestershire, that runs to Bristol; also another in Dorsetshire.*

G.

G Abrantonicorum, G Gabrantorucorum, abrantovicorum,	*Sowerby, or Everley.* *See* Eilimenon.
Sanctus Gabriel in Vico palustri,	*St. Gabriel, Fenchurch Street.*
Gabrocentum, vel Gabrosentum,	*Gateshead, in the Bishoprick of Durham, near Newcastle.*
Gadenii,	*Inhabitants of Teisdate, Tweedale, March, and Lothian, in N. B.*
Gadiva,	*Aberfraw, in the Isle of Anglesey.*
Galva, vel Gallara,	*Walwick, in Northumberland.*
Gallutum, vel Gallagum,	*See* Calacum.
Galatum,	*See* Cacaria.
Gallena, Galera,	*Wallingford, in Berkshire, on the borders of Oxfordshire.*
Galwcia, Gaelwallia, Gallovidia,	*Galloway, in N. B.*
Gangani, Ganganorum,	*People of Connaught, in Ir.*
Gangannum, Langannum promontorium,	*Llyn Promontory, in Caernarvonshire.*
Garbantorigum,	*Caerlaverock, in N. B.*
Gareanorum, Garionum, Garrienis, Ostium,	*Yarmouth, in Norfolk; or rather Burgh Castle, in Suffolk.*
Garrienis, vel Gargenus Flu.	*Yare River, in Norfolk.*
Gausennæ, Gausennis,	*Brig-casterton, in Lincolnshire. See* Cansennis.
Geldeforda, Guldeforda,	*Guildford, in Surrey.*
Genini, Genumia, Genusi,	*See* Ordevices.
Gessoriacum,	*The Streight between Britain and the Isle of Wight.*
Govini,	*A River in Wales that runs into the River Uske.*
Gevissi,	*People over-against the Isle of Wight.*
Girvii,	*Inhabitants of the Fens.*
Glamorgania, vel Glamorgantia,	*Glamorganshire.*

Glannibanta.

Glannibanta, Glanoventa,	*Wentsbeck, or upon the River Wentbeck.*	
Glascovium, vel Glascua,	*Glasgow.*	
Glasconum, Glasconia, Glastonia, Glestonia,	*Glastonbury. See Avalonia.*	
Glastoniensis, Glastingensis,	*Of Glastonbury.*	
Glavorna, Glevum, Glocestria, Gloveceastria,	*Gloucester.*	
Glovernia, Glavornensis provincia, Claudiana provincia,	*Gloucestershire.*	
Glenus Flu.	*The Glen, in Northumberl.*	
Glotta, Glottiana, Clota, vel Cluda,	*The River Clyde, in N. B.; also the Isle of Arran, in the Bay of Clyde.*	
Gobanium,	*See Abergennium.*	
Goderici Castrum,	*Goodrich Castle, in Herefordshire.*	
Granta, Grantanus pons,	*Cambridge. See Camboritum.*	
Granta,	*Supposed to be the River Grant, in Cambridgeshire.*	
Grampius Mons,	*Grantzbain, the Grampian Hills, in N. B.*	
Gravesenda, Greva, Limes prætorius,	*Gravesend, in Kent.*	
Grenovicus, Grenovicum, Greenwicum,	*Greenwich, in Kent.*	
Gnalæ, Guinethia, Gwallia,	*Wales. See Wallia.*	
Guildhalda Tentonicorum,	*The Steel Yard, London.*	
Guerfa Flu.	*The River Wharfe, in Yorkshire.*	
Guldonicus Clivus, Guith,	*Guy-cliff, near Warwick British. See Vecta.*	
Gumicastrum, Gumicaster,	*Godmanchester, near Huntingdon.*	

II.

HABITANCUM, *Rinsingham, in Northumberland.*

Hadriani Murus,	*The Picts' Wall, or Wall of Adrian.*
Haga,	*The Hay, or Hasely, in Brecknockshire.*
Hagulstadia,	*Auston upon Tyne, in Northumberland.*
Hagulstadunum, Hangulstadunum,	*Hangustold, or Hexam, in the Bishoprick of Durham.*
Hagnstaldensis,	*Of Hexam.*
Halenus,	*The River Avon, in Hampshire.*
Hamptonia,	*Southampton. See Clausentum.*
Hansus Flu.	*The River Hans, in Staffordshire.*
Hantonia,	*Hampshire.*
Hastingæ,	*Hastings, in Sussex.*
Hebrides,	*A Cluster of Isles on the West Side of N. B.*
Hebuda, Ebuda, Hebuda prima, Hebuda orientalior,	*Isle of Sky, one of the Hebrides, or Western Isles. in N. B.*
Helenum promontorium,	*The Land's End. See Antivestænm.*
Heliense Cœnobium,	*Ely City, in Cambridgeshire.*
Henlega,	*Henley upon Thames.*
Herculis promontorium,	*Hertey Point, in Devonshire.*
Herefordia, Harefordia,	*Hereford City, in Herefordshire.*
Herefordiæ comitatus,	*Herefordshire.*
Hertfordia, Vadum rubrum, cervinum,	*Hertford.*
Hertfordiæ comitatus,	*Hertfordshire.*
Hesperides,	*The Sorlings, or Scilly Isles.*
Hibernia, Bernia, Ierne, Iernis, Insula Britannica, Inernia, Iris, Inernis, Juverna, Ogygia, Vernia,	*Ireland.*
Hiberniæ, Hibernicus,	*Of Ireland.*
Hinchisega,	*Hinksey, near Oxford.*
Hithinus portus,	*Hithe, in Kent.*

Hodneius

Hoducius Flu.	*Hodney River, in Breck-nockshire, and Bucks.*
Hollandia, Hoilandia, Houlandia,	*Holland, a part of Lincoln-shire.*
Homelea Flu.	*The River Humble, opposite the Isle of Wight, in Hampshire.*
Horesti, Horresti,	*People of Eskdale, in N. B.*
Humbra Flu.	*The River Humber.*
Hullus,	*Hull, in Yorkshire.*
Hundesdena, Hunsdona,	*Hunsdon, in Hertfordshire.*
Hungerforda,	*Hungerford, in Berkshire.*
Hunnum,	*Halton, or Sevenshale, in Northumberland.*
Huntingdonum, Venantodunum,	*Huntingdon Town.*
Huntingdonensis Comitatus, vel Ager Venautodunensis,	*Huntingdonshire.*
Hurstelega,	*Hursley, in Hampshire.*
Hwiccii, Wiccii,	*People of Worcestershire, and about the Severn.*
Hurstanum Castellum,	*Hurst Castle, in Hampshire.*
Huya,	*Holy Island.*
Hymbrionenses, Hymbronenses,	*People of Northumberland.*
Hyrtha,	*The Isle of Hirta.*

I.

JAMESA, Jamissa,	*The Thames, according to Ptolemy. See Tamesis.*
Iccius portus, Itins, Itium Galliæ, Itinus portus,	*Calais Whitsand.*
Iberni, Outerini,	*People of Desmond, in Ireland.*
Sancti Jacobi ad Clericorum Fontem,	*St. James, Clerkenwell.*
Sancti Jacobi ad Ducis Hospitium,	*St. James, Duke's Place.*
Sancti Jacobi ad Montem Allii,	*St. James, Garlick Hyth, or Hill.*
Iceni, Icini,	*People of Suffolk, Norfolk, Cambridge, and Huntingdon shires.*
Iciani, vel Isianos,	*Colchester, also Ickburgh, in Norfolk.*
Idumania,	*The River Stone.*

Idumanum Æstuarium, Idumanus Flu.	*The River Blackwater, in Essex.*
Jena,	*The River Ken, in N.B.*
Ingirvum,	*Jarrow, in the Bishoprick of Durham, where Bede flourished.*
Innerlothea,	*Inverlochy, in N.B.*
Insula,	*Egnesham, or Ensham, in Oxfordshire.*
Insula Siturum.	*The Little Isle of Silley in the Severn.*
Insula Vecta, Vectis, Vectesis,	*Isle of Wight. See Vecta.*
Icta, Intcramna,	*Twintamburne, in Dorset-shire; also Christ-Church, in Hampshire.*
Invernessus,	*Inverness, in N.B.*
Sancti Johannis Baptistæ prope Gall torrentem,	*St. John Baptist, Walbrook, London.*
Isaca, vel Isca,	*The River Ex, in Devon-shire; also the River Esk, in N.B.*
Isamnium, Isanium,	*St. John's Foreland, in Ir.*
Isannium, Isannavantia, Isannavaria, Isannavatia,	*Alcester, Oxfordshire; also Northampton. See Bannavenna.*
Isca Damniorum, Danmoniorum, Dunmoniorum, vel Dunmoniorum,	*Exeter, and Ilchester.*
Isca & Scadum Nunniorum,	
Isca, vel Osca,	*The River Uske.*
Isca Legio 2 Augusta, Iscolegua Augusti, Legio 2 Augusta, Isca Silurum,	*Caerleon City, and Uske, in Monmouthshire.*
Ischalis,	*Inelchester, now Ilchester, in Somersetshire.*
Isiburna,	*Ouseburn, Ousney, or Osney, near Oxford.*
Isidis Insula. Isidis Vadum,	*Oxford. See Oxenforda.*
Isis Flu.	*The River Isis, near Oxford; the Ouse, that runs by Buckingham; another Ouse that runs by York.*
Isuria, Isurovicanus, Isurium, vel Isubriagutium,	*Of Yorkshire. See Eboracensis Agervil Comitatus. Aldborough and Rippon, in Yorkshire.*

Ituma.

Ituma, vel Ituna Flu.	*The River Eden, in West-morland and Cumberland.*
Itunna,	*The River Eden, or Solway Frith, in N. B.*
Itys,	*The River Assin, in N. B.*
Jugantes,	*See Brigantes.*
Juguin Fraxinetum,	*Ashbridge, in Herefordshire.*
Julia Strata,	*A Highway, not far from Caerleon, in Wales.*

K.

KANUS Flu.	*The Kin, in Westmoreland.*
Keneta Cunetio } Flu.	*The River Kennet, in Berk-shire.*
Kerriensis Comitatus,	*The County of Kerry, in Ir.*
Kestevena,	*Kesteven, a part of Lin-colnshire.*
Kildaria, Darensis Episcopatus,	*Kildare, and Kildare Bi-shoprick, in Ireland.*
Kinebantum Castrum,	*Kimbolton Castle, in Hun-tingdonshire.*

L.

LABERUS,	*Killair Castle, in the County of Meath, Ireland.*
Lactodorum, Lactodurum, Lactorodum, Lactorodum.	*Lutterworth, Loughbo-rough, or Bedford; also Stoney Stratford, in Buckinghamshire. See Bedfordia.*
Lacus Ernus,	*Lough Erne, or Iron, in Ir.*
Ladeni,	*See Gadeni.*
Ladensis Episcopatus,	*The Bishoprick of Killalo, in Ireland.*
Lageeium, vel Legiolium,	*Castleford, near Pontefract or Pomfret, in Yorkshire.*
Lamitha, Lomithis. Lonathis,	*Lambeth, in Surrey, near London.*
Lancastria, Loncastria, Longovicum, Longovicium, Lancastrensis Comi-tatus,	*Lancaster, or Lencaster.* *Lancashire.*
Lagenia,	*The Province of Leinster, in Ireland.*
Landava,	*Landaff, in Wales.*
Langanum promon-torium,	*Lheyne Promontory, in Caernarvonshire.*
Lapis Tituli,	*Stonor, in the Isle of Tha-net, in Kent.*
Lavatræ,	

Lavatres, Levatres, Lavatris, Levatris,	*Brough, Westmorland. Browes, upon Stanemore, in Richmondshire.*
Sanctus Laurentius in Judaismo, Sanctus Laurentius Pountnens,	*St. Laurence, Jewry, St. Laurence, Pountney,* } *London.*
Landenia, vel Laudonia,	*Lauden, or Lothian, in N. B.*
Lea Flu.	*The River Lea, in Hert-fordshire.*
Lecheulada, Lechelada, Lathelada,	*Lechlade, in Gloucester-shire.*
Lechlinia,	*Leighlin, in the County of Carlow, Ireland.*
Ledanum, vel Castrum Lodanum,	*Leeds, in Kent.*
Legacestria, Legecestria, Leicastria, Lacestria, Legoria, Legoria Ratæ,	*Leicester, in Leicestershire.*
Legio VI. Nicephoric, Legio VI. Victrix,	*York. See Eboracum.*
Legio XX. Victrix, Legra,	*Chester. See Cestria. The River at Leicester.*
Lelanonius, Levinus,	*Leven River, in N. B.*
Lemanus portus, Lemanii,	*Lime, or Lime-Hill, in Kent.*
Leonense Cœnobium, Leofense, Leorense, Leonis Monasterium,	*Leominster, in Hereford-shire.*
Leonis Castrum,	*Lyons, alias Holt Castle, in Denbighshire.*
Letha,	*Leith Town, in N. B.*
Loegria, Englewria, Englewry, Engleschyria,	*England.*
Levarum,	*Idogher, in South Wales.*
Libnius,	*The River Liffy, that runs through Dublin.*
Lichfeldia, Lychefeldia,	*Lichfield City, in Stafford-shire.*
Licetfeldensis, vel Lecefeldensis,	*Of Lichfield.*
Lideforda,	*Lidford, in Devonshire.* Liddenns,

Liddenus,	*The River Ledden, in Herefordshire, by Malvern Hills.*
Ligu,	*Ligon Isle, on the Coast of France.*
Lelienus, vel Limenus Flu.	*The River Rother.*
Limnos, or Limnus,	*The Isle of Ramsey.*
Limodonus,	*Limehouse, near London.*
Limpida, vel Lympida Sylva,	*Shirewood Forest, in Nottinghamshire.*
Lincolnia, Lindecolina, Lindecollina Civitas, Lindecollinum, Lidocolina, Lindocollinum, Lindon, Lindum, vel Caer-lincoit,	*Lincoln City.*
Lindisfarnia, Lindisfarnum,	*Holy Island, or Farn Isle, on the Coast of Northumberland.*
Lindis,	*The River Witham, in Lincolnshire.*
Lindeseia, Lindisgia, Lindisi,	*Lindsey, a third part of Lincolnshire.*
Linus,	*The River Lin, in Nottinghamshire.*
Linum, vel Linnum Regis,	*King's Lynn, in Norfolk.*
Libœus,	*Sligo Bay, Ireland.*
Lindum,	*Lithgo, in N. B.*
Lisia,	*An Isle called Gulf, near the farthest part of Cornwall.*
Locus Nova Aula,	*Newhall, in Essex.*
Loghor,	*A River, which is the Western Limit of Glamorganshire.*
Logia Flu. vel Logia Rubra,	*Lough Darrige, or the Red Lough, in the North of Ireland, so called from a small Stream which runs over a red Mineral into one Corner of the Lake.*
Logii,	*The People who inhabited from Mount Grampius to the German Ocean; by the Mertæ in N. B.*

Longhas, Louthea, Leutea, Longus Flurius,	*A River on the West Side of N. B. that falls into the Western Ocean; it is called Logh Loug, alias Logh Loughus.*
Longovicum,	*Lanchester, Durham, and Lancaster.*
Londinense oppidum, Londinia, Londinium, Londinum, Londonia, Londinum, Lundonia, Lundonium, Lud-dunum,	*The City of London.*
Louca,	*Goodwin Sands, in Kent.*
Loventium,	*Leveney, in Brecknocksh.*
Loxa,	*The River Lossie, in N. B.*
Luceni, Velabri,	*The People of West Munster.*
Lugas,	*The River Lug, in Herefordshire.*
Luceopibia, Luguballia, Luguballum, Luguvallum,	*Carlisle, Cumberland, and Walwick, Northumb.*
Luva, vel Luda,	*Louth County, in Ireland, and Ludlow, Shropshire.*

M.

Sanctæ Magdalenæ, de Bermcudi Insula,	*St. Magdalen, Bermondsey.*
Sanctæ Magdalenæ in Vico Lacteo,	*St. Mary Magdalen, Milk Street.*
Sanctæ Magdalenæ in Veteri Piscario Foro,	*St. Mary Magdalen, Old Fish Street.*
Sanctæ Margaritæ in Novo Foro Piscario,	*St. Margaret, in New Fish Street.*
Sanctæ Margaritæ à Gallicarum Venditione,	*St. Margaret Pettens,*
Sanctæ MariæAbbatis Ecclesiæ,	*St. Mary Abchurch.*
Sanctæ Mariæ in Aldermannorum Burgo-parochia,	*St. Mary Aldermanbury.*
Sanctæ Mariæ Senioris Mariæ,	*St. Mary, Aldermary,*
Sanctæ Mariæ de Arcubus,	*St. Mary le Bow,*

London.

Sanctæ

Sanctæ Mariæ à Lintris Statione,	St. Mary Bothaw,
Sanctæ Mariæ in Collem,	St. Mary's Hill,
Sanctæ Mariæ de Monte Alto,	St. Mary Mounthaut,
Sanctæ Mariæ de Sabaudiâ,	St. Mary Savoy,
Sanctæ Mariæ ad Lanæ trutinam,	St. Mary Woolchurch,
Sanctæ Mariæ Wolnothi,	St. Mary Woolnoth,
Sancti Martini in Ferrariorum Vienlo,	St. Martin's, Ironmonger Lane,
Sancti Martini ad Luddi Portam,	St. Martin's, Ludgate,
Sancti Martini Ogari,	St. Martin's, Ogars,
Sancti Martini Outwichi,	St. Martin's, Outwich,
Sancti Martini in Vinariis,	St. Martin's, Vintry,
Sancti Michaelis in Hordeaceum Collem,	St. Michael's, Cornhill,
Sancti Michaelis in Curvo Vieulo,	St. Michael's, Crooked Lane,
Sancti Michaelis ad Ripam Reginalem,	St. Michael's, Queen-Hithe.
Sancti Michaelis ad Bladum,	St. Michael's, at the Querne,
Sanctæ Mariæ ad Villam Insularem,	St. Mary. Islington,
Sanctæ Mariæ ad Villam Novum,	St. Mary. Newington,
Sanctæ Mariæ de Alba Capella,	St. Mary, Whitechapel,
Sanctæ Mariæ Salvatoris in Australi opere,	St. Saviour's, Southwark,

London. *Middlesex.*

Madus, Vagniacæ, Vagniacum,	Maidstone, in Kent.
Magæ,—Magi, Maglorœ, Magnæ,—Magni.	Old Radnor, or Old Richmond, Yorkshire.
Magnis.	Cwm, Radnor, Kenchester, and the Gaer, Brecknock. The People of Radnorshire.
Magesetæ, Magnitum, Magioninium, Magiovinium, Magiorintum, Maglona, Maglova.	Dunstable and Sandy, in Bedfordshire.
	Machynlleth, in Montgomeryshire.

Magna,	Chester in the Wall, near Haltwhistle, in Northumberland.
Magnus Portus,	Portsmouth, or Portchester.
Maidulphi Curia, Maidulphi Urbs, Maldunense Monasterium, Malmesburium,	Malmesbury, in Wiltshire. See Bladunum.
Mula Platea,	Ilstreet, in Cheshire.
Malcolicum,	Malk, on the River Shannon, in Ireland.
Mailoria Wallica,	Welch Maylor, or Bromfield, in Denbighshire.
Malvernia, Malvernum,	Malvern, in Worcestershire.
Malus Passus,	Malpas, in Cheshire.
Malcos, Mela. vel Mula,	One of the Hebrides, in N. B.
Mammucinm, Mancunium, Manucium, Manapia,	Manchester, in Lancashire.
	Wexford, in Ireland.
Manduessedum,	Alcester, and Manchester, in Warwickshire, and Mansfield, in Nottinghamshire.
Mannia, Menavia, Menavia Secunda, Mevania, Mona Ulterior, Monabia, Monœda, Eubonia,	The Isle of Man.
Manenses,	The People of that Island.
Manevensis Episcopus	Bishop of the Isle of Man.
Mantavis,	St. David's, Pembrokeshire.
Marchia,	March, in N. B.
Marchidunum,	Roxburgh, in N. B.
Mare Britannicum,	The British Sea.
Mare Sabrinianum,	The Severn Sea.
Marchiæ Walliæ,	The Marches or Borders of Wales.
Margidunum, Margitudum,	Belvoyr, Beauvoir, or Bever Castle, Lincolnshire; also Willoughby, Nott.
Mariduuum, Muriduuum,	Caermarthen. See Caermardinia.
Mariduuensis Ager,	Caermarthenshire.
Mariduuenses, Mureduuenses,	The People of that Shire.
Marlebrigia,	Marlborough.

Marria,

Marria,	*Marr, in N. B.*
Massamensis Pons,	*Masham Bridge, Yorkshire.*
Manditi Castrum,	*St. Mawe's Castle, Cornwall.*
Maxima Cæsariensis,	*Part of England, North of the Humber, and Ribble.*
Mealdunum,	*See Camalodunum.*
Meandari,	*People of Hampshire.*
Meatæ,	*See Hymbrionenses.*
Meanuari, Meaurari,	*Meanborough; Iso Estmean and Westmean Hundreds, in Hampshire.*
Media,—Midia,	*The County of Meath.*
Medweacus,	
Medvaga, Madegvaia,	*The River Medway, in Kent.*
Medena,	*Newport, in the Isle of Wight.*
Mediolanium,	*Middleham, in Yorkshire.*
Mediolanensis,	*Of Lancaster.*
Mediolanum,	*Llanvethlin, or Matrasal, an old Town in Montgomeryshire; also Knightly, in Staffordshire.*
Mediolano,	*Middle Salop.*
Mediterranei Angli,	*See Cornavii.*
Melanclani, Melanchlani,	*People of the Scilly Islands.*
Meldunum,	*Malmsbury, in Wiltshire.*
Meldunensis,	*Of Malmsbury.*
Memma,	*Meneg Isle, Cornwall.*
Menevla, Oppidum Sancti Davidis,	*St. David's, in Wales.*
Merevensis,	*Of St. David's.*
Mercia,	*Middle part of England.*
Mercii,	*—Its Inhabitants.*
Merionithia,	
Mervinia, vel Terra Filiorum Canomi,	*Merionethshire.*
Mersia,	*The River Mersey, in Cheshire.*
Merlebrigia,	*Marlborough.*
Marlebrigia,	*See Cunetio.*
Metaris Æstuarium,	*The Washes, in Norfolk.*
Miba,	*Midhurst, in Sussex.*
Michelnia,	*Michelney, in Somersetshire.*
Middlesexia,	*Middlesex.*
Middletunensis, Mildetunensis,	*Middleton, in Dorsetshire.*
Milfordiensis Portus,	*Milford Haven.*
Milfordia,	*Milford, in Northumberl.*

Modonus,	*The River Arenlisse, in Ir.*
Molis Flu.	*The Mole, in Surrey.*
Mona,	*Anglesey. See Anglesega.*
Menavia,	*The Isle of Man.*
Monasterium de Bello,	*Battle Abbey.*
Monasterium de Mella,	*Meaux Abbey, in Yorkshire.*
Monmuthia,	
Monumetha,	
Monumethia,	*Monmouth, in Wales.*
Monmuthia,	
Monumethensis,	*Of Monmouth.*
Monochapolis,	*Newcastle, in Northumberland.*
Mons Acutus,	*Montacute, in Somersetshire.*
Mons Arenosus, vel Caer Severus,	*Sandon, or Sanbury, in Hertfordshire.*
Mons Dives,	*Richmond, Surrey. See Shenum.*
Mons Gomericus, Montgomeria,	*Montgomery, in Wales.*
Mons Michaelis,	*St. Michael's Mount, in Cornwall.*
Mons Rosarum, Celurca,	*Montrose, in N. B.*
Mons Solis,	*Bath. See Badiza.*
Momonia, Mononia,	*The Province of Munster, in Ireland.*
Moravia, Murevia, Varar, Vararis Æstuarium,	*Murray, and Murray Bay, in N. B.*
Morbium,	*Moresby, in Cumberland.*
Moricamba, Moricambe Æstuarium,	*The Bay of Cardernock, in Cumberland.*
Moridunum, vel Ridunum,	*Seaton, in Devonshire.*
Mortuus Lacus,	*Mortlake, in Surrey.*
Munus,	*The River Munow, that divides Herefordshire from Monmouthshire.*
Murimintum, pro Murivindum,	*Silchester, in Hampshire.*
Murotriges,	*See Darotenses.*
Murus Picticus, Vallum,	*The Picts' Wall. See Hadriani Murus.*

N.

NAESBEIA,	*Naseby, in Northamptonsh.*
Nauticus Sinus,	*Reather, or Rotherhithe, commonly called Redriff.*
	Nemus

Nemus Aquilinum,	*Elstree, or Eaglestree, in Hertfordshire.*
Nemus Boreale.	*North-hall, in Hertfordshire.*
Neomagus, Noiomagus, Noviomagus.	*Guildford. Croydon, and Woodcot, in Surrey: also Holwood Hill, near Bromley, in Kent.*
Neoportus, Novus Portus.	*Newport, in the Isle of Wight.*
Neoportus Paganelli-cus,	*Newport Pagnell, in Buckinghamshire.*
Sancti Nicholai de Ancona,	*St. Nicholas, Acon.*
Sancti Nicholai Aureæ Abbatiæ,	*St. Nicholas, Cole-Abby.*
Nidum, Nidas,	*Neath, in Glamorganshire.*
Nigera,	*Blakeney, in Norfolk.*
Nivicollini,	*Snowdon Mountain, in Caernarvonshire.*
Nordhumbra, Nordhumbri, Northanimbri, Northanimbria, Northinabri, Northinnbria, Northumbria, Nordovolea.	*Northumberland.*
Norfolcia,	*Norfolk.*
Northamptonia.	*Northampton.*
Northantonia,	*See Bannavenna.*
Northantoniensis Ager, vel Comitatus,	*Northamptonshire.*
Northwarthig.	*Derby*
Nortobricum, Nordoricum. Nordovicum.	*Norton Hall, in Yorkshire.*
Norvicum, Norwicus,	*Norwich City.*
Nottinghamia,	*Nottingham.*
Nottinghamiensis Ager, vel Comitatus,	*Nottinghamshire.*
Norantum, Norautum promonto-rinm, Norantum Chersone-sus, Novantii, Novautæ, Novantes, Noriodunum,	*Cockermonth; also the Mul of Galloway, a Promontory in North Britain; and Ardmouth Head there. The Inhabitants in Galloway and Carrick, in N.B. Newenden. See Anderida.*
Norius,	*The Rivers Conway, in Wales; and Nyd, in N.B.*
Novus Burgus,	*Newport. See Medena.*
Norum Castellum, Novum Castrum, Monarchapol,	*Newcastle upon Tyne, in Northumberland.*
Novum Forum, Novum Mercatum.	*Newmarket, in Cambridgeshire.*
Novus Mercatus, Novus Portus,	*Newport, Newhaven, and Rye.*
Nubiria Spiræ, Nuburia,	*Newbury, in Berkshire.*
Nulla ejusmodi, Nulli par, Nulli secunda,	*Nonsuch, in Surrey.*

O.

Obaco,	*The River Liffy, in Ireland.*
Oceanus Virgivus.	*The Virgivian, or Western Ocean.*
Ocetis,	*Hethy Isle, in N.B.*
Occidua Wallia,	*Cornwall. See Corinea.*
Occellum promonto-rium,	*Holderness, also Kelnsey, in Yorkshire.*
Ockhamptonia,	*Oakhampton, in Devonshire.*
Ockus,	*The River Ocke, in Devonshire.*
Ocrinum promonto-rium,	*The Lizard Point.*
Octopilarum promon-torium,	*See Danmoniorum prom. St. David's Head, in Pembrokeshire, in Wales.*
Sancti Olavi, in Cervina Platea,	*St. Olave's, Hart-Street,*
Sancti Olavi, in Australi Opere,	*St. Olave's, Southwark,*
Sancti Olavi, in Argenteo Vico,	*St. Olave's, Silver-Street,*
Omnium Sanctorum de Barking Parochia,	*Allhallows, Barking,*
Omnium Sanctorum in Vico Pistorum,	*Allhallows, Bread-Street,*
Omnium Sanctorum in Vico Longobardico,	*Allhallows, Lombard-Street,*
Omnium Sanctorum in Mellis Viculo,	*Allhallows, Honey-Lane,*
Omnium Sanctorum Pictorum Delibuen-tium,	*Allhallows, Staining,*
Omnium Sanctorum supra Murum,	*Allhallows, the Wall,*

London.

Olenacum,

Olenacum,
Volantium, } *Ellenborough, in Cumberland.*

Olenacum,
Olicana, } *Ilkley, also Halifax, in Yorkshire, and Old Carlisle, Cumberland.*

Orcades Insulæ,
Orchadia,
Orkeneia, } *The Orkney Islands, on the Coast of N. B.*

Ordevices,
Ordoluceæ,
Ordovices, } *People of North Wales.*

Orrea, *A Town on the North of the River Tay, in N. B.*

Ormandia, *Ormond, in Ireland.*
Orus Flu. *The River Ore, in Suffolk.*
Osca, vel
Isca Flu. } *The River Uske, in Wales.*

Osisini,
Osismi, } *People of France, towards the British Sea.*

Ostæi,
Ostiones, Ostidumni, } *People of Cornwall and Devonshire. See Damnonii.*

Ostium Sturæ, *Stourmouth, in Kent.*
Ottadeni,
Ottadini,
Ottalini,
Ottatini,
Ottodani, } *People of Northumberland. See Hymbrionenses.*

Ottaforda, *Otford, in Kent.*
Othonia, *See Ad Ansam.*
Ousa,—Oza,
Usa, } *Ouse River, in Yorkshire, and in Buckinghamshire.*

Ovinia Insula,
Insula Ovium, } *Isle of Sheppey, in Kent.*

Oxenforda,
Oxfordia,
Oxonia,
Oxonium, } *Oxford City.*

Oxinaga, *Oxney Isle, in Kent.*

P.

PALUS SALSA, *Pulhely, in Caernarvonshire.*

Sancti Pancrasii in
Vico Smegmatico, } *St. Pancras, Soper's Lane.*

Parathalassia, *Walsingham, in Norfolk.*
Parisi, *People of Holderness, in Yorkshire.*

Sancti Pauli in Conventuali Horto, } *St. Paul's, Covent-Garden.*

Pegelandia,
Pembrochia, } *Peckirke, near Crowland.*
Pembroke, in Wales.

Pendinas, } *Pendennis Castle, in Cornwall.*

Penguernum, *Shrewsbury Town, in Shropshire.*

Penlinnia, } *A place in Merionethshire, where the Lake Tagit is, whence rises the River Dee.*

Pennocrucium,
Pennocrutium, } *Stretton, Penkridge, and Oldbury, Staffordshire.*

Pennorinum, *Penrith, in Cornwall.*
Pente Flu. *The River Pant, in Essex.*
Perscora,
Persora, } *Pershore, in Worcestershire.*

Peterillus,
Peterus Flu. } *The Peterill, in Cumberland.*

Petrianæ, *Castle Steeds, or Cambeck Fort, Cumberland.*
Petrianæ, *Penrith. See Voreda.*
Petriburgus,
Petropolis, } *Peterborough City, in Northamptonshire.*

Petuaria, } *Brough, on the Humber; and Beverley, in Yorkshire.*

Sancti Petri in Foro, *St. Peter's, Cheap.*
Pevensea, *Pevensey, in Sussex.*
Pictavia,
Pictandia, } *The Country of the Picts.*

Picti, } *The Picts, a People of Britain.*

Placentia, *A Palace at Greenwich, built by Humphrey, Duke of Gloucester.*

Plymutha, *Plymouth.*
Plinlimonia,
Pontana, } *A high Mountain of Drogheda, in Ireland.*

Pontes, } *Wynardsbury, and Colnbrook, Bucks; Reading, Berks; and Dorking, in Surrey.*

Pons Ælii, } *Ponteland, in Northumberland.*

Pons Burgensis, *Boroughbridge, in Yorkshire.*

Pons Elii, *Pont-Eland, in Northumberland.*

Pons Fractus, *Pomfret, or Pontefract, in Yorkshire.*

Pontuobici, or
Punctuobici, } *Cowbridge, Glamorganshire.*

Pontus

Pontus Flu.	*The Point, in Northumberland.*
Populorum Lapis,	*Folkstone, in Kent.*
Portesmutha,	*Portsmouth.*
Portus Magnus,	*See Magnus Portus.*
Portus Ostium,	
Portus Lemanis,	*Lime, in Kent.*
Portus Britanniarum,	*Portsmouth, and Richborough, in Kent.*
Portus Sistuntiorum,	*Bargerode, near Poulton, Lancashire.*
Portlandia,	*Portland Isle.*
Portunia Insula,	
Portus Ammonis,	*Sandwich. See Sabulovicum.*
Portus Dubris,	*Dover.*
Portus Salutis,	*Cromarty, in Scotland.*
Povisia,	
Powisa,	*Powis, part of Wales.*
Powisia,	
Præsidium,	*Warwick Town.*
Prætorium,	*Patrington, in Yorkshire.*
Prestona,	*Preston, in Lancashire.*
Procolitia,	*Pruddoe, or Pruddoe Castle, in Northumberland.*
Protolitia,	
Profundum Vadum,	*Deptford.*
Putenega,	*Putney, in Surrey.*
Pulchrum Vadum,	*Fairford,in Gloucestershire.*

R.

RADECOTANUS Pons,	*Radcot Bridge, in Oxfordshire.*
Radnoria,	*Radnor, in Radnorshire.*
Radnoriæ Comitatus,	*Radnorshire.*
Raga,	
Ragæ,	*Ratiford, or Radford.*
Raganeia,	
	Ralegh, in Essex.
Ramesburia,	*Ramsbury, in Wiltshire, or Ramsey, in Huntingdonshire; also Brinklow, Warwickshire.*
Ramesia,	
Rataæ,	*Leicester. See Legacestria.*
Ratæstabius Flu.	*The River Tave, in Glamorganshire; also the River Abertivy, in Wales.*
Ratostabius,	
Rhatostatibius,	
Ratostathybius,	
Readingum,	*Reading, in Berkshire.*
Regiodunum Hullinum,	*Kingston upon Hull, in Yorkshire.*
Regiodunum Thamesinum,	*Kingston upon Thames.*
Regis Burgus,	*Queenborough, in Kent.*

Regis Comitatus,	*King's County, in Ireland.*
Regui,	*People of Surrey, Sussex. and the Sea Coasts of Hampshire.*
Regnum,	*Chichester, Sussex.*
Regni Sylva,	*Ringwood, in Hampshire.*
Reculsum,	*Reculver, in Kent.*
Regulbium,	
Repandunum,	*Repton, in Derbyshire.*
Rerigonium,	*Ribchester, Lancashire; and Bargenny, in Scotland. See Berigonium.*
Rherigonium,	
Rhetigonium,	
Rhedus Flu.	*The Read, in Northumberland.*
Rhemains,	*The River Remny, in Glamorganshire.*
Rhibellus Fln.	*The Ribble, in Lancashire.*
Rhitubi Portus,	
Rhntubi Portus,	
Rhutupiæ Statio,	
Rhitupus Portus,	
Rhitupis Portus,	
Rhitupius Portus,	*Replacester, Ruptimuth, Richberg, now Richborough, near Sandwich, in Kent.*
Rutupinus Portus,	
Rutupinum Littus,	
Rutupiæ,	
Rhutupiæ Trutulensis Portus,	
Rutupius Portus,	
Rutupinæ Urbs,	
Rhius,	*The River Rie, in Yorkshire.*
Rhobogdium promontorium,	*Fair Foreland, in Ireland.*
Rhobogdii, vel Vennicnii,	*People of Donegal, or Tyrconnel, in Ireland.*
Rhobodunum,	*Ribchester, in Lancashire; Richmond, or Rippon, Yorkshire. See Coccium. or Guccium.*
Ribodunum,	
Rigodunum,	
Richmondia,	*Richmond, in Yorkshire; also Richmond,in Surrey. See Shenum.*
Richmundia,	
Ricinia,	
Ricina,	*Racline Isle, the least of the Hebrides, and next to Ireland.*
Rieluna,	
Ricnea,	
Riduna,	
Ripadium,	*Repton, in Derbyshire.*
Ripandunum,	
Ripodum,	*Rippon, in Yorkshire.*
Robertinus Pons,	*Rother Bridge, in Sussex.*
Rodecotanus Pons,	*Radcot Bridge, on the River Isis, in Oxfordshire. Roibis,*

Roibis, Roffa.	} Rochester, in Kent. See Darvernorum.
Roisie oppidum,	Royston, in Cambridgeshire.
Rossia,	{ Rosse-Land, in Cornwall; Rose, in Pembrokeshire; also a Bishoprick in N.B.
Rothesia,	{ The Island of Rothsay, which formerly gave the Title of Duke to the Prince of Scotland: now called the Isle of Bute, or Bute, near Galloway, in N.B.
Rugnitunia, Ruitonia, Rutunia,	} Riton upon Dunsmore, in Warwickshire.
Ruber Clivus.	{ Redcliffe, near London, vulgarly called Radcliffe, or Ratcliffe.
Rupes Fergusii,	Northjergus, in Ireland.
Rupis Aurea,	{ Goldcliffe, in Monmouthshire.
Ruthunia, Rutlandia,	Ruthin, in Denbighshire. Rutlandshire.
Rutunium,	{ Rowton and Wroxeter, in Shropshire.
Rutupia,	Richborough, Kent.
Rutupirum Littus, Rutupiæ,	} The Foreland of Kent.

S.

SABAUDIA.	The Savoy, in London.
Sabriana, Sabrina, vel Saverna.	} The River Severn.
Sabulovicum.	
Sandicum, Saudovicus, Sanwicum,	} Sandwich, in Kent.
Sacana,—Sena, Senus,—Siambis, Sineus,—Socinos,	} The River Shannon, in Ireland.
Sacra Insula,	{ Holy Isle, by Northumberland.
Sacra Bosco, Sacra Sylva,	} Halifax, in Yorkshire.
Sageolium,	Doncaster, in Yorkshire.
Salenæ, Salinæ,	} Salndy, in Bedfordshire.

Salesburia, Salisburia, Salopesbiria, Salopia, Saresberia, Sarisburia, Severia,	} Salisbury City, in Wiltshire.
Salimnos Insula,	{ Sulmey Isle, near Milford Haven.
Salopesbiria, Salopia, Scrobberia, Scorberia, Scrobbesbiria, Scorbesberia, Slopesbaria, Salopiæ Comitatus.	} Shrewsbury, in Shropshire. See Penguernum.
Saltria,	{ Shropshire. Sawtry, in Huntingdonshire.
Saltus Andreda,	{ The Weald of Kent, according to Verstegan; Wald, Weald, and Wold, signify one thing, viz. a Wood or Forest.
Salutaris Portus, Sinus Portuosus & Salutaris,	} Sowerby, or Everley. See Eilimenon.
Salwarpus.	{ Salwarp River, in Worcestershire.
Samothea.	{ Britain. See Albion.
Sarnia,	Guernsey Island.
Sceptonia,	Shaftsbury, in Dorsetshire.
Schelsega,	Chelsea, near London.
Schirburnia,	{ Sherborne. See Clara Fontanus.
Scona,	{ Scone, in N.B. The place where the Kings of Scotland were crowned.
Scoti,—Scotus.	The Scots.
Scotia,	{ Scotland, now North Britain.
Sebasta, Altera Legio,	} Liskeard, in Cornwall.
Secandunum,	{ Seckington, in Warwickshire.
Segodunum,	{ Seaton, or Sedghill, in Northumberland.
Segelocum, Segelogum,	{ Aulert in Shirwood, in Nottinghamshire; Agle, and Ancaster, in Lincolnshire; Littleborough, in Nottinghamshire.
Segontiaci,	

Segontiaci, Segontium,	*Caernarvon, and Cair-se-jont, near it.*	Southeriensis, Sudriensis, Southregienses,	*Of Surrey. See Regni.*
Segnntium,	*Silchester.* *See Marimintum.*	Southsexena, Southsexia, Sussexia,	*The County of Sussex.*
Selburgi Tumulus,	*Sebury Hill, in Wiltshire.*		
Sengennetb,	*Caerphilly, Glamorganshire.*	Southwella,	*Southwell, in Nottingham-shire.*
Seolesia, Silesia,	*Seolsey, or Selsea, in Sus-sex; also a Bishop's See.*	Spea,	*The River Spey, in N.B.*
Setantiorum Palus,	*Winander Mere, in Lanca-shire.*	Spinarum Insula, vel Thornega,	*Thorney Isle, the old name of Westminster.*
Setcia Æstuarium.	*Dee-mouth.*	Spinæ.—Spiney,	*Newbury, Reading, and Thatcham, in Berkshire.*
Sharpernoria.	*Sharpnore, in the Isle of Wight.*	Staffordia, Stanfordia,	*Stafford Town.* *Stamford, in Lincolnshire.*
Shenum,	*Shene, or Richmond, in Surrey.*	Stata Florida,	*Strat-flower, or Strat-fleur, in Cardiganshire.*
Sigdeles, Sillinæ Insulæ.	*The Isles of Scilly.*	Sancti Stephani, in Vico Columanni,	*Saint Stephen's, Coleman Street.*
Silionnus,	*Ramsey Isle.* *See Limnos.*	Stenum,	*Stene, in Northamptonshire.*
Silura,	*The little Isle of Silley in Severn. See Camden.*	Stonrus, Starus durus,	*The River Stour, in Kent, in Dorsetshire, and in Suffolk.*
Silures,	*People of South Wales.*	Streanshall Monastery	*Ancient Name of Whitby Abbey.*
Sinnodunum,	*Sinnsdun-Hill, near Wal-lingford, in Berkshire.*	Stratfordia Stenica,	*See Lactodorum, &c.*
Sitomagus, Simomagus,	*Thetford; also New Boken-ham, in Norfolk.*	Strigulia, vel Stringulia,	*Chepstow, in Monmouth-shire.*
Sinomagus,	*See Tedfordia.*	Strivillina.	*Stirling, in N. B.*
Slepa,	*The old name of St. Ives, in Huntingdonshire.*	Stuccia, vel Stucia Flu.	*Ystwith, in Cardiganshire.*
Snawdonia,	*Snowden Forest, in Caer-narvonshire.*	Sturodunum,	*Stourton, and Stourminster, in Dorsetshire.*
Solvathianum Æstua-rium,	*Solway Frith, in N. B.*	Sturus Flu.	*The Stour, in Derbyshire.*
Somaridunum,	*Somerton, in Lincolnshire.*	Sualva, Swala,—Isis,	*River Swale.* *See Cataracta Flu.*
Somersata, Somerseta, Somersetania, Somersetensis, vel Somertunensis Comi-tatus,	*Somersetshire.*	Suirus,	*Showre River, near Water-ford, Ireland.*
		Snlealva Flu.	*The Swale, in Yorkshire.*
		Sudoverca, Sudovolca,	*Southwark.*
Sorbiodunum, Sorviodunum, Soruroduunu,	*Old Sarum, or Salisbury.*	Suffolcia, Suffolicia,	*Suffolk.*
Southamptonia,	*Southampton.* *See Clausentum.*	Suelloniaca, Sultonica, Sullimaca,	*Brockley-Hill, near Elstree, in Hertfordshire; also Barnet, or Edyworth Sheuley.*
Southantunensis,	*Of Southampton.*	Sumotriges,	*See Dorotenses.*
Southeria, Southriona, Southria,—Sudria, Sunderheia, Surria,—Suthria, Suthriona,	*County of Surrey.*	Sunningum, Swiftus,	*Sunning, by Reading.* *Swift River, in Leicester-shire.*

T.

TADECASTRUM,   *Tadcaster.* *See Cacaria.*

Taffus Flu.   { *The River Taaf, in Glamorganshire. See Ratæstabius Flu.*

Taizales,   } *People of Northumberland.*
Taizalos & Vernicones, } *See Hymbrionenses.*

Taizalum promonto- } *Buchanness, in N. B.*
rium,

Taizali,   { *The People of Buguham, or Buchan, in N. B.*

Tama Flu.   { *The River Tame, in Oxfordshire; another in Staffordshire.*

Tama oppidum.   { *Thame, a Town in Oxfordshire.*

Tamara   }
Tamaras } Flu.   { *The River Tamar, in Cornwall.*
Tambra   }

Tamare,   *Tavistock, Devon.*
Tamara oppidum,   *Tamarton, in Cornwall.*

Tamawordina,   }
Tamworthia, } *Tamworth, in Staffordshire.*

Tamesis,   }
Tamensis, } { *The River Thames, and the*
Tamisis, } { *Medway. See Jamexa.*
Thamisis,   }

Thamesis,   { *The River Thames; also Moulsford, Berks.*

Tamesa Æstuarium, } *Mouth of the Thames.*
vel Tamæsa,

Tanathos   }
Teno   }
Thanatos } Insula.   *The Isle of Thanet, in Kent.*
Thanaton }
Toliapis   }

Tanfelda,   *Tanfield, in Yorkshire.*
Tava,   *Teignmouth, Devon.*

Tavus,   { *The River Tay, and South Esk, in N. B.*

Tavistokia,   *Tavistock, in Devonshire.*
Taurus,   *Tur River, in Devonshire.*

Tæsobius,   }
Toisobius, } { *The River Conway.*
Toisovius, } { *See Conovius.*

Tedfordia,   { *Thetford, in Norfolk.*
Theodfordum,   { *See Sitomagus.*

Tetfordensis,   }
Thetfordensis, } { *Of Thetford.*

Theta,   { *The River on which Thetford stands.*

Tesa,—Teisis,—Tæsis } *The River Tees, in the Bi-*
Teisa,—Tuesis, } *shoprick of Durham.*

Tegæus Lacus,   { *The Lake Tagit, or Pemble Mere, in Merionethshire, in Wales.*

Terentus   }
Trehenta } Flu.   *The River Trent.*
Trenta   }

Tetoenria,   *Tetbury, in Gloucestershire.*

Theobaldenses Ædes, { *Theobald's House, in Hertfordshire.*

Theodorodunum,   *Wells, in Somersetshire.*

Theoci curia,   } *Tewkesbury, in Gloucester-*
Theokesberia, } *shire.*

Thermæ,   *Bath. See Aquæ Calidæ.*

Thongum,   { *Thong Castle, in Lincolnshire.*

Thonodunum,   *Taunton, in Somersetshire.*

Thornega,   { *Thorneye, or Thorney Isle, the old name of Westminster.*

Tisobis,   *The River Conway.*
Thorneia,   *Thorney, in Cambridgeshire.*

Thule,   }
Tile, vel } { *Supposed to be the Shetland Isles.*
Ultima Thule, }

Thuetmonia,   } *Thomond, in Ireland.*
Tomondia, }

Titchfelda,   *Titchfield, in Hampshire.*

Tina,—Tinna,— } Flu. { *The River Tyne, in North-*
Tinus,—Thinus } { *umberland.*

Tidolana,   *Winchester in the Wall.*

Tinemutha,   }
Tinnocellum, } { *Tynemouth, in Northumber-*
Tunnocellum. } { *land.*
Tunocellum,   }

Tintagium,   *Tintagell, in Cornwall.*
Tolapia,   *Isle of Sheppey.*

Toliapis,   } { *See Ovinia Insula.*
Toliatis, }

Trajectus Augustæ, { *Aust Passage, Gloucestershire.*

Torcestria,   } *Towcester, in Northampton-*
Tripontium, } *shire.*

Tripontium,   *Edge Hill, Warwickshire.*
Totonesium,   *Totness, in Devonshire.*
Trenovantum,   *See Londinense oppidum.*
Trimontium,   *Atterish, a Town in N. B.*

Trinoantes,   }
Trinobantes, } { *The People of Middlesex and Essex.*
Trinovantes,   }

Trisantona,   { *The River Test, that runs into Southampton Bay.*
                                   Trisantou,

Trisantou,
Trisantonis Portus, } *Southampton.*
 See Clausentum.
Tuesis. *Berwick. See Abrevicum.*
Tueda,—Tuesis. } *River Tweed.*
Tweda,—Twedum, } *See Barvicus.*
 Inchtuthill, a City of the Picts, formerly situated on the Banks of the River Tay, in N. B., but destroyed in the Roman Wars, according to Hector Boëthius.
Tulina,
Turobius, *The River Tave, in Wales.*

V.

VACOMAGI. { *People of Murray, in Scotland.*
Vadum Pulchrum, *See Pulchrum Vadum.*
Vaga, vel } Flu. { *The River Wye, in Herefordshire.*
Waga. { *Rochester, Wrotham, and Southfleet, in Kent.*
Vagniacæ,
Vagniacum, *Maidstone. See Madus.*
Vallis Aurea. { *Golden Vale, in Herefordshire.*
Vallis Crucis. { *The Vale of the Cross, in Denbighshire.*
Vallis Anangia, *Annandale, in N. B.*
Vallum. { *The Picts' Wall.*
 { *See Hadriani Murus.*
Vandalis Flu. { *The River Wandle, in Surrey.*
Vandelbiria, { *Wandlesbury, a Fort on the Hills, near Cambridge.*
Vanatinga, *Wantage, in Berkshire.*
Varia Flu. *The Frome, in Dorsetshire.*
Varis. *Banjary, in Flintshire.*
Vecta.—Vectis,
Vectesis,—Victesis, } *The Isle of Wight.*
Vecturiones, *The Scots. See Scoti.*
Vedra,—Vedrus, *River Wear. Durham.*
Veluntium, *Argles, in Ireland.*
Venantodunia. *Huntingdonshire*
Venantodunum,
Venantorum Mons. } *Huntingdon Town.*
Venedotia. *North Wales.*
Veneti. *People of Britany, in France.*
Venonæ, { *High Cross, Claybrooke, Leicestershire.*
Venta Belgarum, } *Winchester, in Hampshire.*
Venta Simenorum,

Venta Icenorum, { *Castor, Norwich; also Brancaster, in Norfolk.*
Venta Silurum, { *Caer-went, in Monmouthshire.*
Vennicujum promontorium, } *Ramshead, a Promontory in Ireland.*
Vergivium Mare. *See Oceanus Virgivus.*
Verlucio. { *Devizes; also Warminster, Westbury, and Leckham, in Wilts.*
Vernonatum, *Leicester.*
Vernemetum.
Vernametum. } { *Burrow Hill, in Leicestershire, and near Willoughby, Nott.*
Verometum,
Verolamium,
Virolamium,
Verulaminum, } { *The ancient City of Verulam, now St. Alban's, in Hertfordshire.*
Verulanium,
Urolaminm,
Urolanium,
Venonis.—Benonis,
Verovicum. } *The Town of Warwick.*
Vervicum,
Warwicus,
Veruvium, *St. Andrew's Cape, in N. B.*
Vetelegamus Pons. { *Wheatley Bridge, near Oxford.*
Vernicones, { *People of Northumberland; also of Mernis, in N. B.*
Verteræ,
Verteris, } { *Burgh upon Stanemore, in Westmorland; also Old Penrith, Cumberland.*
Vetus Burgus, *Elvert, in Durham.*
Vertilingiani Via.
Via Consularis. } *Watling Street Way.*
Vexala, vel } *Juellmouth, in Somersetshire.*
Uzela Æstnarium, }
Viconia, { *Binchester, and Ebchester, Durham. See Binonium.*
Vinonium,
Vinovia,
Vinovium,
Vicus Malbanus. *Nantwich, in Cheshire.*
Vicus Orientalis. *Eastwick, in Hertfordshire.*
Vicus Saxeus, { *Standrop, or Stainthorp, in the Bishoprick of Durham.*
Victoria,
Vidogara, } { *Inch Keith Isle, in the Shire of Ayr, N. B.*
Viervedrum,
Virvedrum, } { *Dunsbey, or Duneansbey, one of the three Northern Promontories of N. B.*
Vigornia, *Worcester. See Branovium.*
Villa Faustini,
Villa Regia, } { *Malden, in Essex; also St. Edmundsbury, in Suffolk.*
 Villa

H

Villa Nova,	Newenham, in Hertfordshire.
Villa Novi Castri super Tinam,	Newcastle upon Tyne.
Vilugiana Provincia,	Wiltshire. See Wiltonia.
Vinchelsoga, Vindagora,	Winchelsea, in Sussex.
Vindelis, Vindelisora,	Old Winchelsey. Windsor, in Berkshire.
Vindobala, Vindomora,	Rutchester on the Wall, or Wall's-End, in Northumberland.
Vindogladia, Vindugladia,	Greenchester, Winborne, & Badbury. See Winburna.
Vindolana,	Old Winchester, in Northumberland.
Vindomis, Vindonum, Vindonus,	Silchester. See Murimintum.
Vinduglessus,	Venicles, or Gaunless, a Rivulet in the Bishoprick of Durham.
Virecinum, Vireeium, Virioconium, Viroconium, Uriconium, Uriconia,	Wroxeter, in Shropshire.
Viridis Sinus, Viridusinus,	Wrottesley, Staffordshire. Greenwich. See Grenovicus.
Virosidum,	Warwick upon Eden, near Carlisle, in Cumberland.
Visi Saxones,	West Saxons.
Vitrea Insula,	Glastonbury. See Avalona.
Viluli Insula,	Selsea. See Seolesia.
Vodiæ & Udiæ Congani,	People about Cork.
Voldia,	Cotswold, in Gloucestershire.
Voliba,	Bodmin, in Cornwall.
Voluba,	Falmouth, or Valemouth, in Cornwall.
Volucrum Domus, vel Amius,	Fulham, in Middlesex.
Voluntii, Darni,	People of Ulster, in Ireland.
Voreda,	Old Penrith, Carlisle, Vorran, and Plumpton, in Cumberland.
Ubbanforda,	Norham, in Northumberland.

Ulearus,	The Isle of Oleron. Here Richard the First compiled the Great Roll of Oleron from the Rhodian Laws. The Inquisition at Quinborough, 49 Ed. III. was but a Rehearsal and Confirmation of those Laws; as the Jurisdiction of the Lord Admiral was long before the reign of Ed. III. See Selden's Mare Clausum, 222, 254, & Co. Litt. sect. 234.
Ulidia, Ultonia, Hultonia.	The Province of Ultagh, or Ulster, in Ireland.
Ulmetum,	Elmeley, Yorkshire.
Univallis, Urivallis,	Jorval, in Yorkshire.
Uriconium,	Wroxeter, Shropshire.
Urosullum,	Wressall, in Yorkshire.
Urovicum,	York. See Eboracum.
Urus,	The River Ouse, in Yorkshire.
Usocona, Usoconna, Uxacona,	Okenyate, or Oaken Gates, in Shropshire.
Uxela,	Wall, Lichfield; Staffordshire: Crekehorn, or Crackern Well, Devon.
Uxinus Pons,	Uxbridge, in Middlesex.
Uzella,	Lostwithiel, in Cornwall.

W.

WAKEFELDIA,	Wakefield, in Yorkshire.
Waldenses,	Tenants of the Manor of Darenth, Kent.
Walkenested,	Godstone, Surrey.
Wulani, Wallenses,	Welchmen.
Waldena, Wallia,	Saffron Walden, in Essex. Wales.
Wara,	The Town of Ware, in Hertfordshire.
Warvicus,	Warwick.
Warwicana Provincia, Warwici Comitatus,	Warwickshire.
Weableia, Winbleia,	Weobly Town, in Herefordshire.

Welandus.

Welandus,	{ Welland River, in North- amptonshire.	Wilsati, Wiltenses,	} People of Wiltshire.
Wellæ.	{ Wells City, in Somerset- shire.	Winundhamia, Winburna,	Wynundham, in Norfolk. Wimborne, in Dorsetshire.
Weulanus,	Of Winchester.	Winceleumba,	} Winchcombe, in Gloucester-
Weutana Civitas,	} Winchester.	Wincheleumba.	shire.
Wincestria,	See Venta Belgarum.	Winchelsega,	See Vinchelsega.
Weskus.	Wesk River, in Yorkshire.	Windesora,	
Westberia,	Westbury, near Bristol.	Windlesora.	} Windsor, in Berkshire.
Westmaria,		Windesoria.	
Westmoria,	} Westmorland.	Wintonia,	Winchester.
Westmorlandia,		Wirus,	{ Wear River, Bishoprick of Durham.
Westmonasterium, Visimonasterium.	} Westminster City.	Wrekus,	{ Wreck River, in Leicester- shire.
Wetha, vel	{ Isle of Wight.	Witlesia,	{ Whittlesea, in Huntingdon shire.
Wotha,	See Vecta.		
Weverus.	{ The River Wever, in Che- shire.		
Wiburti Villa,	Wiberton.		
Wichcombia,	{ Wickham, in Buckingham- shire.		
Wichum,	Wick, in Worcestershire.		
Wiccia,			
Wiccii,	} Worcestershire.	**Y.**	
Wigornia Comitatus.		YARUM,	Yarm, in Yorkshire.
Wigornia,	Worcester. See Branovium.	Yarienis, Garienus,	} Yare River, in Norfolk.
Wilda, vel	} The Wild of Sussex.	Yarmuthia,	
Walda Sussexiæ,		Jernmuthia,	
Wilfarus Dun,	{ Didderston, or Diddersley Hall, Yorkshire.	Garanonum, Garienis Ostium,	} Yarmouth, in Norfolk.
Wiltonia.	Wiltshire.	Yoogeriecenstric, pro	} Worcester. See Concilia,
Wiltunensis,	Of Wilts.	Wiogrecenastere,	per Spelman, 433.

ALPHABETICAL TABLE

OF

ANCIENT SURNAMES,

AS THEY WERE WRITTEN IN OLD DEEDS, CHARTERS, AND RECORDS.

A.

DE Adurni portu,	*Etherington.*
de Albencio,	*D'Aubeney, Albiney.*
de Alba Marla,	*Albemarle.*
Albericus,	
Albren,	
Albræns, vel	} *Awbrey.*
Aubericus,	
de Albo Monasterio,	*Whitchurch.*
Ala Campi,	*Wingfield.*
Henricus de Alditheleia,	} *Was the first Lord Audley.*
de Alneto,	*Dauney.*
de Arenbus,	*Bowes.*
de Alta ripa,	*Dautry.*
de Aqua frisca,	*Freshwater.*
Aquapontanus,	*Bridgwater.*
de Arida villa,	*Dryton, or Drydon.*
Arundelius,	
Arundelius de Hirundine,	} *Arundel.*
Johannes Avonius,	*John of Northampton.*
de Auco,	*Owe.*
Aurifaber,	*Orfeur, an ancient name in Cumberland.*
de Aula,	*Hall.*
de Aureo vado,	*Goldford, or Guldeford.*

B.

BARDULPHUS,	
de Batonia,	} *Bardolph.*
de Beaumois,	
de Belesmo,	
de Beda, vel	} *Bacon.*
de Bajocis,	
de Bella aqua,	*Bellew.*
de Bella fide,	*Beaufoy.*
de Bello loco,	*Beaulieu.*
de Bello foco,	*Beaufeu.*
de Bello marisco,	*Beaumarsh.*
de Bello fago,	*Beaufo.*
de Bello campo,	*Beauchamp.*
de Bello monte,	*Beaumont.*

de Bello prato,	
de Bensto,	} *Beaupre.*
de Beverlaco,	
de Bello situ,	*Bellasise.*
de Benefactis,	*Benfield.*
Benevolus,	*Benlows.*
de Bona villa,	*Bonevil.*
de Bono fossato,	*Goodrick.*
de Blostevilla,	*Blovile, Blofield.*
Blaunpain, alias	} *Whitbread.*
Blanepain,	
Bononius,	*Bollen.*
Borlasius,	*Borlace.*
de Bortani, sive	} *Burton.*
Burtana,	
de Bovis Villa,	*Bovil.*
de Bosco,	} *Bois.*
de Braiosa,	
de Bosco Roardi,	*Borhard.*
de Bruera,	*de Bryer, or Bryer.*
de Bulinco,	{ *Bussi, or Bussey. One of this name founded Blyth-Abbey, Anno 1088.*
de Burgo,	*Burgh, Burk, or Bourk.*
de Burgo charo,	*Bourchier.*

C.

DE Calvo monte,	*Chaumond.*
de Camera,	*Chambers.*
de Campania,	*Champneis.*
de Campo Florido,	{ *Champfleur, Henry de Campo Florido was Sheriff of Dorsetshire, 19 Hen. III.*
de Campo Arnulphi,	*Champernoun.*
de Capricuria, &	} *Chevercourt.*
de Capreolocuria,	
de Cantilupo,	*Cantlow, or Cantello.*
de Camrilla,	*Camvil.*
de Capella,	*Capel.*
Caradocus,	{ *Caradock, or Cradock, now called Newton.*
de Caro loco,	*Carelieu.*
de Casa Dei,	*Godshall.*

de Casineto.

de Casineto, & Chais- neto, }	*Chedney, Cheney.*
de Castello,	*Castle, or Castel.*
de Castello magno,	*Castlemain.*
de Ceraso,	*Cherry.*
de Cestria,	*Chester.*
Cinomannicus.	*Maine.*
de Chauris & Cadurcis,	*Chaworth.*
Cheligrerus,	*Killigrew.*
Chirchebeius,	*Kirby.*
de Claro monte.	*Clermont.*
de Claris vallibus, Claranas. }	*Clarival, or Clare.*
de Clarifagio,	*Clerfey.*
de Clintona.	*Clinton.*
de Clivo forti,	*Clifford.*
de Columbariis.	*Columbers.*
de Conductu,	*Chenduit.*
de Cornubia.	*Cornwayle.*
de Corvo Spinæ.	*Crowthora.*
de Curva Spina,	*Creithorne.*
de Crepito Corde, de Curevo, de Curci, de Cusancia, }	*Creveo, or Creveceur.*
Cunctins,	*Kenet.*

D.

DE Dalenrigius, de David villa.	*Dalegrig.* *D'Aieille, D'Eyville.*
D'Ayuccuria, vel Daincuriensis, }	*Daincourt.*
de Dovera,	*Dover.*
de la Mara.	*De la Mare.*
de Doito (Fr. Doet),	*Brooke.*
Dispensator,	*Le Despencer, Spencer.*
de Diva,	*Dive, Dives.*
Drogo (Saxon),	*Drew.*
Dunestanvilla.	*Dunstavile.*
Dutentius,	*Doughty.*

E.

DE Ebroicis, & de Ebrois, }	*D'Eereux.*
Easterlingus,	*Stradling.*
Tho. de Erolitto,	{ *Erliche. He was Sheriff* *of Salop 6th of King* *John.* }
de Ericeto,	*Briewer.*
Estlega, & de Estlega, }	*Astley, or Estley.*
Extraneus,	*L'Estrange.*

F.

DE Fago,	*Beech and Beecher.*
de Ferrariis,	*Ferrars.*
de Filiceto,	*Fernham.*
Filius Alani,	*Fitz-Alan.*
Filius Alvredi,	*Fitz-Alard.*
Filius Amandi,	*Fitz-Amand.*
Filius Andreæ,	*Fitz-Andrew.*
Filius Bernardi,	*Fitz-Barnard.*
Filius Brinni,	*Fitz-Brian.*
Filius Comitis,	*Fitz-Count.*
Filius Eustachii,	*Fitz-Eustace.*
Filius Fulconis,	*Fitz-Fulk.*
Filius Galfredi,	*Fitz-Geofry.*
Filius Gerrardi,	*Fitz-Gerrard.*
Filius Gilberti,	*Fitz-Gilbert.*
Filius Guidonis,	*Fitzwith.*
Filius Hardingi.	*Fitz-Harding.*
Filius Haimonis,	*Fitz-Haimon.*
Filius Henrici,	*Fitz-Henry.*
Filius Herberti,	*Fitz-Herbert,*
Filius Hugonis,	*Fitz-Hugh.*
Filius Humphredi,	*Fitz-Humphry.*
Filius Jacobi,	*Fitz-James.*
Filius Johannis,	*Fitz-John.*
Filius Lucæ,	*Fitz-Lucas.*
Filius Mauricii,	*Fitz-Maurice.*
Filius Michaelis,	*Fitz-Michael.*
Filius Nicholai,	*Fitz-Nichols.*
Filius Oliveri,	*Fitz-Oliver.*
Filius Osburni,	*Fitz-Osburn.*
Filius Osmondi,	*Fitz-Osmond.*
Filius Otonis.	*Fitz-Otes.*
Filius Pagani,	*Fitz-Pain.*
Filius Patricii,	*Fitz-Patrick.*
Filius Petri,	*Fitz-Peter.*
Filius Radulphi,	*Fitz-Ralph.*
Filius Reginaldi,	*Fitz-Raynold.*
Filius Ricardi,	*Fitz-Richard.*
Filius Roberti,	*Fitz-Robert.*
Filius Rogeri,	*Fitz-Roger.*
Filius Simeonis,	*Fitz-Simon.*
Filius Stephani,	{ *Fitz-Stephen, commonly* *called Stephenson.* }
Filius Thomasi,	*Fitz-Thomas.*
Filius Walteri,	*Fitz-Walter.*
Filius Warreni,	*Fitz-Warren.*
Filius Gulielmi,	*Fitz-William.*
de Foliis,	*Foulis.*
de Fonte Australi,	*Southwel.*
de Fonte limpido,	*Sherburn.*
de Fontibus,	*Wells.*

de Fonte

de Fonte Ebrardi,   *Fontererard.*
de Forti scuto,   *Fortescue.*
Flavus,   *Blund, Blount.*
de Fossa nova,   *Newdike.*
de Fluctibus,   *Flood.*
Frescobarnus,   *Freshburne.*
de Frisca Marisco,   *Freshmarsh.*
de Frevilla,   }
de Frisca villa,   } *Frevil, or Fretchvile.*
de Fraxino,   *Frene, Ashe.*
de Fronte bovis,   *de Grundbeof.*

G.

DE Gandavo, &   }
    Gandavensis,   } *Gaunt.*
de Glanvilla,   *Glanvil.*
de Gorniaco,   *Gorney, or Gurney.*
de Granavilla, vel   }
    Greenvilla,   } *Greenvil, or Grenvile.*
de Grandavilla,   *Granvile.*
de Geneva,   *Generile.*
de Genisteto,   *Bromfield.*
de Grendona,   *Greendon.*
Giovannis,   *Young.*
de Grosso Venatore,   }
Grandis, vel   } *Grosvenor.*
Magnus Venator,   }
de Grosso monte,   *Grismond.*
de Guntheri sylva,   *Gunter.*

H.

DE Hantona,   *Hanton.*
    de Harcla,   *Harkley.*
Havertus,   }
Howardus,   } *Howard.*
de Hosata,   }
Hosatus, vel   } *Hose, or Hussey.*
Usus Mare,   }

I.

JODOCUS,   *Joice.*
    de Insula,   *Lisle.*
de Insula bona,   *Lislebone.*
de Insula fontis,   *Lilburne.*
de Ipra,   *de Ipres.*

K.

DE Kaineto, alias   }
    Caineto,   } *Keynes.*

L.

DE Laga,   *Lee, Lea, and Leigh.*
    Lambardus,   *Lambard, or Lambert.*
de Langdona, vel   }
    Landa,   } *Langdon.*
de Lato campo,   *Bradfield.*
de Lato vado,   *Bradford.*
de Lato pede,   *Bruidfoot.*
de Lato loco,   *Lettley.*
de Leicestria,   *Lester.*
Le Leica, & Lecha,   *Leke.*
Leuchenovus,   *Lewkin.*
de Lexintuna,   *Lexington.*
Laurentii filius,   *Lawson.*
de Limesi,   *Limsie.*
de Linna,   *Linne.*
de Lisoriis,   *Lizurs, Lisors.*
de Logiis,   *Lodge.*
de Longo campo,   *Longchamp.*
de Longo prato,   *Longmede.*
de Longa spata,   *Longspee.*
de Longa villa,   *Longville.*
Lupus,   *Woolf, Love, Loo.*
Lupellus,   } *The Family of Lovel, or*
                       } *Lovet.*

M.

MACER,   *Le Meyre.*
    de Mala platea, & } *Malpas.*
de Malo passu,   }
Magnus Venator,   *Grosvenor.*
de Magna Villa, &   }
de Mandavilla,   } *Mandeville.*
de Magroomonte,   *Grosmount or Groumount.*
de Mala terra,   *Manland.*
de Malis manibus,   *Malmains.*
Malus catulus,   *Mulchein, vulgo Machel.*
de Malo lacu,   *Mauley.*
Male conductus, vel   } *Malduit.*
de Malo conductu,   }
de Malo leone,   *Malleon.*
de Malo visu,   *Malvisin.*
Malus leporarius,   { *Maleverer, Mallieure, com-*
                       {   *monly Mallyvery.*
Malus lupellus,   *Manlovel, Mallovel.*
de Maneriis,   *Manners.*
de Marchia,   }
Marisca,   } *March, or Marsh.*
Marisco,   }
Marescallus,   *Moreschal, or Marchal.*
de Marci vallibus,   *Martival.*
de Meduana,   *Maine.*
de Media villa,   *Middleton.*
                                    de Melsa.

de Melsa,	Mews.
Mediens,	Leech.
de Micenis,	Meschines.
de Mineriis,	Miners, or Minours.
de Molendinis, Molendinarius,	} Mulines.
de Moelis,	Malles.
de Monasteriis,	Masters, or Masters.
Monachus,	Moigne, Monk.
de Monte canisto,	Montchensey.
de Monte hermerii,	Monthermer.
de Monte fixo,	Montfitchet.
de Monte pessono,	
de Monte pessulano,	} Montpesson, vulgo
Monte pissonis, vel	} Mompesson.
de Monte pissoris,	
de Monte Jovis,	} Montjoy.
de Monte Gaudii,	
de Monte acuto,	Montacute.
de Monte alto,	Montalt, or Mould.
de Monte Gomericæ,	Montgomery.
de Monte-begonis,	Monthegon.
de Monteforti,	Montfort.
de Monte aquilæ,	Mounteagle.
de Mortuo Mari,	Mortimer.
ad Murum,	Walton.
de Musco campo,	Muschamp.
de Mowbraia,	Mowbray.

N.

DE Nevilla, & de Nova villa,	} Nevil.
Nigellus,	Niele, or Neal.
de Novo burgo,	Newburgh.
de Novo loco,	Newark.
de Novo castello,	Newcastle.
de Nodariis, vel Nobriis,	} Nowres.
Norriscus,	Norris.
de Norwico,	Norwich.
de Nova Terra,	Newland.
de Novo mercatu,	Newmarch.

Q.

DE Oileio, & Oili, & Oilius,	} D'Oily.

P.

PAGENELLI,	Paynells, or Painels.
de Pavilliano, Pietonus,	} Peiton.
de Parva villa,	Littleton.

Parmentarius,	Taylor.
de Palude,	Puddle, Marsh.
de Pascua Capidoso,	Stanley.
de Pavilidro, & Fauliaco,	} Paveley.
de Pede planco,	Pauncefoot.
de Peccato,	Peche, vel Perke.
Pelliparius,	Skinner.
de Perrariis,	Perrers.
de Petraponte,	{ Pierrepont, vulgarly { Perpoint.
de Pictavia,	Peyto.
de Plantageneta,	Plantagenet.
ad Pontem,	Paunton.
de Porcellis, vel Purcellis,	} Purcell.
Le Ponre,	Power.
de Praeriis,	Praers.
de Pulchro capellitio,	Fairfax.
de Putenco,	Pusae, commonly Pudsey.

Q.

DE Quereeto,	Cheney.
de Quinciato,	Quincey.

R.

DE Ralega, vel Regencia,	} Raleigh.
de Radeona,	Rodney.
de Redveriis, de Repariis, Rigidii, de Riperia,	} Rivers.
Reginaldus,	Reynolds.
de Rico Monte,	Richmond.
Rotarius,	Wheeler.
de Rubra spatha,	Rouxearrier, Roussie, Rooper, Roper. There is a very ancient Family of the Ropers in Cumberland, who have lived immemorially near a Quarry of Red Spate there, from whence they first took the Surname of Rubra Spatha.
de Rupe forti,	Rochfort.
de Rupe, Rupibus, Rupinus,	} Roche, Rock.
de Rubro clivo,	Radcliff.
de Rubra Manu,	Redmain.
Rusus,	Rous.
de Rupe scissa,	Cuteliffe

S.

DE Sabaudia,   Savoy.
  de Sacra quercu,   Holyoak.
de Sacra fago,   Hollebech.
de Sacra bosco,   Holywood.
de Sacra fonte,   Holybrook.
de Saio,   Say.
Sagittarius,   Archer.
de Salecto,   Saucey.
de Salicosa mara,   Wilmore.
de Salchavilla,   Salkeld.
de Salicosa vena,   Salvein.
de Salso marisco,   Saltmarsh.
de Saltu capellæ,   Sacheverel.
Salvagius,   Savage.
de Sancto Mauro,   St. Maur, or Seymour.
de Sancto Lando,   Sentlo, or Senlo.
de Sancta Terra,   Holyland.
de Sancta Clara,   St. Clare, Seneleer, Sinclair.
de Sancto Medardo,   Semark.
de Sancto Amando,   St. Amond.
de Sancto Albano,   St. Alban.
de Sancto Audomaro,   St. Omer.
de Sancto Lizio, &   } Seuliz. Seyton.
  Sylvaneclensis,
de Sancta Ermina,   Armine.
de Sancta Fide,   St. Faith.
de Sancto Mauricio,   St. Morris.
de Sancto Wallerico,   St. Wallere.
de Sancto Leodegario,   St. Leger, vulgo Sallenger.
de Sancta Barbara,   Senbarb, vulgo Simberb.
de Sancto Petro,   Sampier.
de Sancto Paulo,   Sampol, or Sample.
de Sancto Lupo,   Sentlowe.
de Sancto Audœno,   St. Owen.
de Sancto Gelasio,   Singlis.
de Sancto Martino,   Semarton.
de Sandwico,   Sandwich.
de Sancto Quintinio,   St. Quintin.
de Sancto Alemondo,   Salmon.
de Sancto Vedasto,   Foster.
de Saxo ferrato,   Ironston, vulgo Ironzon.
de Scalariis,   Scales.
de Sicca villa,   Drytown, or Sackvile.
Sitfiltu, alias Cecilius,   Sitfilt.
de Solariis,   Solers.
de Spineto,   Spine.
de Stagno,   Poole.
de Stipite sicco,   De la Zouch.
de Stratone,   Stretton.
Super Tysam,   Surteys.
de Sudburia,   Sudbury.

de Suthlcia, &   } Suthley, or Sudley.
  Sutlcia,
de Sylva,   Weld.

T.

DE Tanaia,   Taney.
  de Tankardi villa,   Tankerville.
Teutonicus,   Teys.
de Tulka,   Toke, Tuke.
de Turbida villa,   Turberville.
Turchetissus,   Turchill.
de Turri,   Towers.
de Parva Turri,   Torel, Tirrel
de Turpi Vado,   Fulford.

V.

DE Vado Saxi,   Stanford.
  de Vado boiim,   Oxford.
de Valle torta,   Vautort.
de Valle,   Wale.
de Valentia,   Valence.
de Vallibus,   Vaux.
de Vesci,   Vesey.
de Veteri aula,   Oldhall, Oldham.
de Veteri ponte,   Vipont, or Vipount.
de Vicariis,   Viccars.
de Villa torta,   Croketon.
de Villariis,   Villers.
de Villa magna,   Mandevile.
de Vino salvo,   Vinesalf.

de Umbrosa quercu,   Dimouk, now Dimmock. This ancient Family have performed the Office of Champion to the Kings of England ever since the Coronation of Richard II., as holding the Manor of Scrivelsbury hereditarily, from the Marmions of Lincolnshire, by Grand Serjeantry — so adjudged M. 1 Hen. VIIth.

de Urtico.   Lorti, Lort.

W.

DE Warrenna,   Warren.

de Warnevilla, vel   } Willoughby.
  Willoughbæus,
de Watelega,   Wateley. Wheatley.

EXPOSITION

OF

LATIN WORDS,

FOUND IN THE LAW OR OTHER ANCIENT WRITINGS, BUT NOT IN ANY MODERN
DICTIONARY OR GLOSSARY.

A.

ABATARE,	To abate.
Abatamentum,	Abatement.
Abbatia,	} An Abbey.
Abbathia,	
Abeyancia,	Abeyance.
Abcariare,	To carry away.
Abettum,	} Abetment.
Abbettum,	
Abbettator,	An Abettor.
Abbettare,	To abet.
Abjudicare,	To forejudge.
Abjudicator,	A Forejudger.
Abbuttare,	To abut.
Abuttans,	Abutting.
Accessarium,	Accessory.
Accustumatus,	
Accustomatis,	} Accustomed.
Accustomabilis,	
Accomplimentum,	Accomplishment.
Acetiam, vel Acceiam,	And also.
Acquietancia,	An Acquittance.
Acquietare,	To acquit.
Litera acquietancialis,	Letters of acquittal.
Acquisitum,	
Adquisitum,	} A Purchase.
Perquisitum,	
Adjacencia,	Things adjoining.
Adjornare,	To adjourn.
Adjornamentum,	Adjournment.
Admirallus,	Admiral.
Admiralitas,	Admiralty.
Adnullare,	To annul.
Adnullatio,	Annulling.
Advantagium,	An Advantage.
Advanceamentum,	An Advancement.
Adrentura,	An Adventure.
Adventurare,	To adventure.
Advisare,	To advise.
Advisamentum, vel	} Advice.
Avisamentum,	
Advocatio,	An Advowson.
Avocare,	An Avowry.
Aeria accipitrum,	An Aery of Hawks.

Afferatores,	Affeerors.
Afferatus,	Affeered.
Afforestare,	To afforest.
Affri,	Plough Cattle.
Affraia,	An Affray.
Affreatamentum,	A Freightment.
Affrectatus,	Freighted.
Agistare,	To agist.
Agistamentum,	An Agistment.
Agreare,	To agree.
Agreamentum,	An Agreement.
Aisamentum,	An Easement.
Aldermannus,	An Alderman.
Alteragium,	Alterage.
Allottatus,	Allotted.
Alterare,	To alter.
Alteratio,	An altering.
Amerciamentum,	An Amercement.
Amerciatus,	Amerced.
Amortizare,	To amortize.
Amortizatio,	An Amortization.
Amotibilis,	Removeable.
Anchoragium,	Anchorage.
Apparentia, vel Comparentia,	} An Appearance.
Appellum,	An Appeal.
Appellare,	To appeal.
Appellans,	An Appellant.
Appellat,	An Appellee.
Appendicium,	A Dependance, an Addition.
Apportionare,	To apportion.
Apportionamentum,	An Apportionment.
Apprenticius,	An Apprentice.
Apprentisagium, vel Apprenticiamentum,	} An Apprenticeship.
Appropriatio,	} An Appropriation, or Im-
Appropriamentum,	propriation.
Appropriare,	To appropriate.
Approbator, vel Probator,	} An Approver.
Approbare,	To approve.
Apprnare,	To improve.
Appruamentum,	An Improvement.

i   Decime

Decime de Aracijs Equorum,	Of the Races (or Breed) of Horses.
Aranatus,	Arraigned.
Aranamentum,	An Arraignment.
Arrainare Assisam,	To arraign an Assize.
Arbitrator,	An Arbitrator.
Arbitrium, vel Awardium,	An Award or Arbitrement.
Archa in claustro,	An Arch in a Cloister.
Archeria,	Archery.
A retro & insolutus,	Behind and unpaid.
Armirarij linearum arniturarum,	Armorers of Linen Armory; Merchant Taylors of London.
Arraiare,	To array.
Arraiamentum,	An Array.
Arraiatores,	Arrayers.
Arrectatus, rectatus,	Suspected, accused.
Arrentare,	To rate.
Arrentatio,	A Rate or Rent.
Arreragia,	Arrearages.
Arrestare,	To arrest.
Arrestum,	An Arrest.
Arrivare,	To arrive.
Articulare,	To article.
Articulus,	An Article.
Arurae, Messurae, Falcationes,	Earings, or Plowings, Mowings, Reapings.
Assaia & Assisa Panis,	The Essay and Assize of Bread.
Assartum, vel Essartum,	An Assart.
Assartare,	To assart.
Assemblare,	To assemble.
Assemblatio,	An Assembly, or Assembling.
Assisa,	An Assize.
Assuare, vel Assecurare,	To assure.
Assurantia,	An Assurance.
Attachiare,	To attach.
Attachiamentum,	An Attachment.
Attemptare, Attentare,	To attempt.
Attincta,	An Attaint.
Attinctus,	Attainted.
Attornatus,	An Attorney.
Scriptum Attornatorium,	A Letter of Attorney.
Attornare,	To attorn.
Attornamentum,	An Attornment.
Averaginm,	Average.
Averia,	Cattle.

Avisamentum,	Advice.
Avisatus,	Advised.

B.

BACCALAUREUS, Artium,	A Bachelor of Arts.
Baga,	A Bag.
Baga de secretis,	The Place where the Attainders are kept in the Upper Treasury of the King's Bench.
Bagea,	A Badge.
Baia,	An Haven.
Ballancea,	A Balance.
Ballium,	A Bail.
Ballivus,	A Bailiff.
Balliva,	A Bailiwick.
Balus,	A Bale of Goods.
Bancus,	A Bench.
Banda Militaris,	A Band of Soldiers.
Banna,	Bans of Matrimony.
Bannerium,	A Banner.
Bannerettus,	A Banneret.
Bannitus,	Banished.
Bannitio,	A Banishment.
Barcaria,	A Tan-house, Sheep-house, or Heath-house.
Barca,	A Bark.
Barellus,	A Barrel.
Barga, vel Bargea,	A Barge.
Barganizare,	To bargain.
Bargania,	A Bargain.
Barganizatio,	A Bargaining.
Baro,	A Baron.
Baronia,	A Barony.
Baronettus, vel Baronatus,	A Baronet.
Barra,	A Bar to an Action.
Barrectator,	A Barretor.
Barratria,	Barratry.
Bartona,	A Barton.
Bassus,	Low.
Bastardus,	A Bastard.
Bastarda, vel Bastardia,	Bastardy.
Batus,	A Boat.
Batellus,	A little Boat.
Beconagium,	Beconage.
Bedellus,	A Bedel.
Beneficium,	A Benefice.
Beneficiatus,	Beneficed.

Billio,

Billio, vel
Bullio, } *Bullion.*

Billettum, { *A Bill, or Billet, of Deli-*
very of a Writ.

Blada, *Corn.*
Terre Bladate, *Corn Land.*
Bogetta, *A Budget.*
Boscus,
Boscaria, } *Wood growing, a Wood.*
Bosculus, *A little Wood.*
Botha, *A Booth or Stall.*
Botava terre, *An Oxgang of Land.*
Boveria, *An Ox-house.*
Borarij, *Ox-keepers.*
Boviculus, *A Bullock.*
Breve. *A Writ.*
Broccator, *A Broker.*
Brocarij, *Brokers.*
Brocagium, vel
Broctagium, } *Brocage.*
Bruera, *Heath Ground.*
Bullaria aque salse, *A Bullery of Salt Water.*
Bultellum, *Refuse of Meal.*
Bunda, *A Bound.*
Bundellus, *A Bundle.*
Burgagium, *A Burgage.*
Burglaria, *A Burglary.*
Burgus, *A Borough.*
Burgensis, *A Burgess.*
Bursarius, *The Bursar of a College.*
Busca, *Hedging Wood.*
Butta, *A Butt.*

C.

CALCETUM,
Via calceata, } *A Causeway.*

Calcifurnium, *A Lime Kiln.*
Calendarium, *A Table, or Repertory.*
Calendare, *To make Repertories.*
Calumniare, *To challenge.*
Calumnia, *A Challenge.*
Cambi partia, *Champarty.*
Cambi particeps, *A Champertor.*
Cambium, *A Change.*
Cambire denarium, *To change Money.*
Literie Cambitorie, *Letter or Bill of Exchange.*
Camera,
Cameralis, } *A Chamber.*
Campio, *A Champion.*
Canopium, *A Canopy.*
Cancellare, *To cancel.*
Cancellatura, *A Cancelling.*

Cappa, *A Cap.*
Capa, *A Cape.*
Capellania,
Capellaria, } *A Chapelry.*
Capitaneus, *A Captain.*
Capitulum. *A Chapter.*
Decanus&Capitulum, *A Dean and Chapter.*
Carcare, *To Freight.*
Carcatus, *Freighted.*
Caristia, *Dearness.*
Caruca, *A Cart.*
Carectata, *A Cart-Load.*
Caruca signata. *A Car-Room.*
Carrus, { *A Car, Coach, or Cha-*
riot.
Cariare, *To carry.*
Cariagium, *A Carriage.*
Cassare, *To quash.*
Cassatio, *An Abatement.*
Catalla, *Chattels.*
Celda, *A Chaldron.*
Chacea, *A Chase.*
Chaciare, *To chase or drive.*
Cigninota, *A Swan Mark.*
Cirographum finis, *The Chirograph of a Fine.*
Circumhabitantes, *Near-dwellers.*
Civilista, *A Civil Lawyer.*
Clameus, *A Claim.*
Clamare, *To claim.*
Clava, *A Mace.*
Clerimonia, *Privilege of Clergy.*
Cloca, *A Clock.*
Clocarium, *A Clock House or Case.*
Coadunatio, *An assembling together.*
Cofeoffati, *Joint Feoffees.*
Cofera,
Coferis, } *A Coffer.*
Coferarius, *A Cofferer.*
Cognitor, *A Connsor.*
Cognizatus,
Cognizarius, } *A Conusee.*
Cognitio, *A Cognizance.*
Coiso, *A Coif.*
Baro de Gradu de } *A Baron of the degree of*
la Coife, *the Coif.*
Cokettum, *A Coket.*
Cokettatus, *Coketed.*
Collecta Ovium, *A Flock of Sheep.*
Collecta Bladi, *A Heap of Corn.*
Colonellus, *A Colonel.*
Comfortare, *To comfort.*
Comitiva, vel Comita- } *A Band or Troop of Sol-*
tiva Soldariorum, *diers.*

Commensare.

Commensare,	To commence.
Commensatio,	A Beginning.
Commensalis,	A Border.
Commensale,	Board or Diet.
Communiarius,	A Commoner.
Pro communibus, Pro commensali,	Commons in an Inn of Court.
Commissio,	A Commission.
Commissionarius,	A Commissioner.
Communia Pasture,	Common of Pasture.
Communia Turbarie,	———— Turbary.
Communia Estoverio-rum,	———— Estovers.
Communia Piscarie,	———— Fishery.
Communiare,	To common.
Compassare,	To compass.
Concelare,	To conceal.
Concelamentum,	A Concealment.
Concernere,	To concern.
Concernens,	Concerning.
Concernatus,	Concerned.
Conquestus, Conquestari,	A Conquest.
Constabularius, Constabularia, Constabulariatus,	A Constable.
Contignatur,	Is near.
Contrariare,	To do contrary.
Contraplacitum,	A Counter-plea.
Contraveniens,	Offending, going against.
Contrivare,	To contrive.
Controfacere,	To counterfeit.
Controfactura,	A Counterfeiting.
Controllamentum,	A Controlment.
Contrarotulator,	A Comptroller.
Contrarotulus,	A Counter Roll.
Conveiare,	To convey.
Conveiancia,	A Conveyance.
Coopertura,	A Covering, a Coverture.
Coparcenaria,	Coparcenary.
Coparticeps,	A Coparcener.
Copia,	A Copy.
ad Copiandum,	To copy.
Copicia,	A Coppice.
Corda,	A Cord or String.
Corda ligni,	A Cord of Wood.
Cornerium, Angulus,	A Corner or Angle.
Costera Maris,	The Sea Coast.
Costera Montis, Summitas Costere,	The surrounding Mountains or Hills.
Cotagium,	A Cottage.

Cotarius, Coterellus,	A Cottager.
Covina,	Covin or Fraud.
Covinosus,	Fraudulently, deceitfully.
Cranare,	To crane.
Cranagium,	Cranage.
Creca, Crecum,	A Creek.
Croftum,	A Croft.
Coinaginm, Cunagium,	Coinage.
Cuneus,	Coin.
Cunicularium,	A Rabbit-Warren, or Place to keep Rabbits in.
Curtilaginm,	A Curtilage.
Curtina,	A Curtain.
Custagium, Custus,	Costs.
Custuma,	Custom for Wares.
Custumaria tenementa,	Copyhold.
Tenentes Custumarij,	Copyholders.

D.

DAMMA,	A Dam.
Data,	The Date of a Deed or Writ.
Deadvocare,	To disavow.
Debatum,	A Debate.
Decanus,	A Dean.
Decanatus,	A Deanery.
Decenna,	A Tything.
Decennarius,	A Tythingman.
Decimatio,	Tything.
Decime,	Tythes.
Declarare,	To declare.
Declaratio,	A Declaration.
Defalta,	A Default.
Defeasancia,	A Defeasance.
Deforciare,	To deforce.
Deforciator,	A Deforcer.
Deforciamentum,	A Deforcement.
Demanda,	A Demand.
Demandare,	To demand.
Denarata Redditus,	A Penny Rent.
Denarata Olei,	A Pennyworth of Oil.
Denizatus,	A Denizen.
Departura,	A Departure.
Departire,	To depart.
Depasturare,	To depasture.
Depasturatio,	A Depasturing.
	Desponsalia.

Desponsalia,	Marriage.	Escaetor,	An Escheator.
Devisare,	To devise.	Escaeta,	An Escheat.
Devisum,	⎫	Escurare,	To scour.
Devisatio,	⎬ A Devise, or Devising.	Escripta,	Escripts.
Devisamentum,	⎭	Esculenta.	Meat.
Dimidium unius Acre,	⎱ Half an Acre.	Poculenta,	Drink.
vel Dimidia Acra,	⎰	Eskippare,	To skip.
Dimidia Hida,	Half an Hide of Land.	Establiamentum,	An Establishment.
Dirationare,	To disprove.	Estallagium,	An Instalment.
Dirationamentum,	A Disproof.	Estoveria,	Estovers.
Discarcare,	To unlade.	Estrepamentum,	Estrepement.
Dishabilitare,	To disable.	Evidentia,	Evidence.
Disseisire,	To disseise.	Excambium,	An Exchange.
Desseisina,	A Disseisin.	Excambire,	To exchange.
Disseisitor,	A Disseisor.	Excambiator,	An Exchanger.
Disparagare,	To disparage.	Exclusa,	A Sluice.
Disparagatio,	A Disparagement.	ExclusagiaMolendini,	⎱ The Mill Sluice.
Disturbare,	To disturb.	vel Emissarium,	⎰
Disturbatio,	⎱	Expirare,	To expire.
Disturbancia,	⎰ A Disturbance.	Expiratio,	An Expiring, or Ending.
Divisa,	A Bound.	Explesias, vel	⎱ Profits.
Dividenda,	A Dividend.	Explees,	⎰
Divorcium,	Divorce.	Extenta,	An Extent.
A diu,	For a long time.	Extortio,	Extortion.
Dola, vel Dolea,	A Dole.	Extorsive,	Extorsively.
Dominicum,	Demesne.	Extorta pecunia,	Money extorted.
Donator,	⎱ A Donor.		
Donatorius,	⎰		
Donatus,	A Donee.	**F.**	
Draparius,	A Draper.		
Drana,	A Drain.	FALDA,	A Fold.
		Faldagium,	Foldage.
		Fardella,	A Fardel.
E.		Farundella terre,	⎱ A Farundel or Fardel of
			⎰ Land.
EBBA,	An Ebb.	Felo,	A Felon.
Ebba & Fluctus,	⎫	Felo de se,	A Felon of himself.
Fluvius & Ebba,	⎬ Ebb and Flow of the Tide.	Felonia,	Felony.
Flumen & Ebba,	⎭	Felonice,	Feloniously.
Effectualis,	Effectual.	Fensura,	A Fence.
Effectualiter,	Effectually.	Feodum,	A Fee.
Elargare,	To enlarge.	Feodarius,	A Feodary.
Elargatio,	⎱ An Enlargement.	Feodi firma,	A Fee Farm.
Elargiamentum,	⎰	Feoffamentum,	A Feoffment.
Emenda,	⎱ An Amends.	Feoffator,	A Feoffor.
Emende,	⎰	Feoffatus,	A Feoffee.
Endurare,	To endure.	Feria,	⎱ A Ferry, or a Fair. Spel-
Engrallatus,	Ingrailed, 1 Mon. 930.		⎰ man, 264.
Enitia Pars,	⎰ The Elder Sister's Part of	Ferlingata terre,	⎱ A Quarter of a Yard-Land.
	⎱ Lands.	Ferdellum terre,	⎰
Equitatura,	Travelling Furniture.	Fidelitas,	Fealty.
Escapia,	An Escape.	Filare,	To File.
Escapiare,	To escape.	Filacium,	A File.
		Filazarius,	A Filazer.

Filum

Filum aque.	*The Middle of the Breadth of a River.*
Finare,	*To refine.*
Finis,	*A Fine, or Concord of Land, for an Income of Lands, for an Offence.*
Firma,	*A Farm.*
Firmarius,	*A Farmer.*
ad Firmam tradere,	*To let to farm.*
Flotans,	*Floating.*
Flota Navium,	*Fleet of Ships.*
Focale,	*Fuel.*
Focagium,	*Hearth Money.*
Foderum,	*Fodder.*
Foragium,	*Forage.*
Fodera Plumbi,	*A Fodder, or Fother of Lead.*
Fogagium,	*Fog.*
Forcia,	*Force.*
Foresta,	*A Forest.*
Forestarius,	*A Forester.*
Forgea,	*A Forge.*
Forisfacere,	*To forfeit.*
Forisfactura,	*A Forfeiture.*
Forma,	*A Form.*
Forprisa,	*A Foreprise.*
Forprisatus,	*Foreprised.*
Forstallare,	*To forestal.*
Forstallator,	*A Forestaller.*
Forstallamentum,	*A Forestalment.*
Fortunare,	*To happen.*
Fossatum,	*A Ditch.*
Framea, Fabrica,	*A Frame.*
Franchesia,	*A Franchise.*
Franchisatus,	*Enfranchised.*
Francus Bancus, vel Francbordus,	*Free-Bench.*
Visus Franci Plegij,	*View of Frank-Pledge.*
Friscus Mariscus, Mariscus Friscus,	*Fresh Marsh.*
Terra jacens frisca & ad warrectum,	*Land lying fresh and fallow.*
Frustrare,	*To make void.*
Frustratoria dilatio,	*Useless or unnecessary Delay.*
Furlongus,	*A Furlong.*
Furnitura,	*Furniture.*

G.

GALO, Galona,	*A Gallon.*
Gaola,	*A Jail.*
Gaolarius,	*A Jailor.*

Garba,	*A Sheaf.*
Garcio,	*A Page.*
Garderoba,	*A Wardrobe.*
Garderobarius,	*A Wardrobe-keeper.*
Garlanda,	*A Garland.*
Garterium,	*A Garter.*
Gistum,	*Yeast or Barm.*
Globa,	*A Globe.*
Terra Globalis,	*Globe Land.*
Graduatus,	*A Graduate.*
Grangia,	*A Grange.*
Grometus, vel Valletus,	*A Groom.*
Grossum,	*A Gross.*
Grossus,	*Gross.*
Grova,	*A Grove.*
Grovetta,	*A little Grove.*
Guarda,	*A Ward.*
Guardianus,	*A Warden.*
Guerra,	*War.*
Modo guerrino,	*In warlike Manner.*
Guilda,	*A Guild or Fraternity.*
Gunna,	*A Gun.*
Guttera, vel Guttura,	*A Gutter.*

II.

HAIA,	*A Quickset Hedge.*
Hamlettum, Hamleta,	*A Hamlet.*
Hanaperium,	*A Hamper.*
Harepipa,	*An Harepipe.*
Haspa,	*An Hasp.*
Hatchettus,	*An Hatchet.*
Heraldus,	*An Herald.*
Herbagium,	*Herbage.*
Herciare,	*To harrow.*
Hereditas,	*An Inheritance.*
Hereditamenta.	*Hereditaments.*
Heriotum,	*An Heriot.*
Hernesia, vel Harnesia,	*Harness.*
Hida terre, Hidagium,	*An Hide of Land.*
Hitha,	*An Hythe.*
Homagium,	*Homage.*
Hundredum,	*An Hundred.*
Hundredarius,	*An Hundredor.*
Husbandria,	*Husbandry.*
Hustingus,	*An Husting.*
Hutesium & clamor,	*Hue and Cry.*

J.

JAMPNUM,	*Furze or Gorse.*
Jampnorum,	*Of Furze.*
Imbesilare,	*To imbesil.*
Imbreviare,	*To reduce into Schedules or Writing.*
Impannellare,	*To impannel.*
Imparcare,	*To impound.*
Imparcamentum,	*Impounding.*
Imperpetuum,	*For ever.*
Impetere,	*To impeach.*
Impetitio,	*An Impeachment or Hindrance.*
Implementa,	*Implements.*
Implacitare,	*To implead, to sue.*
Impoisonare,	*To poison.*
Importancia,	*Importance.*
Imposterum,	*Hereafter.*
Imprisa, Interprisa,	*An Enterprize.*
Imprisonare,	*To imprison.*
Imprisonamentum,	*An Imprisonment.*
Includere,	*To inclose.*
Inclausura,	*An Inclosure.*
Incombrare,	*To incumber.*
Incombrancia,	*An Incumbrance.*
Incrochiare,	*To incroach.*
Incurramentum,	*An Incurring.*
Indebitatus,	*Indebted.*
Indefesibilis,	*Indefensible.*
Indefensus,	*Undefended.*
Indentura,	*An Indenture.*
Indictare,	*To indict.*
Indictamentum,	*An Indictment.*
Indistringibilis,	*Not distrainable.*
Indivisum,	*Held in common, not divided.*
Infossatus,	*Ditched in.*
Ingrossare,	*To ingross.*
Ingrossator,	*An Ingrosser.*
Inlagatio,	*Inlawing.*
Inlagatus,	*Inlawed.*
Inquestum,	*An Inquest.*
Inquisitio,	*An Inquisition.*
Instaurare,	*To stock.*
Instaurum,	*A Stock.*
Instauramentum,	*Stocking.*
Instaurata terra,	*Stocked or improved Land.*
Intantum,	*So much, so far.*
Intercommunicare,	*To intercommon.*
Interpugnare,	*To fight together.*
Invadiare,	*To mortgage.*
Invadiatio,	*A Mortgaging.*

Inventarium, Inventorium,	*An Inventory.*
Investitura,	*An Investiture.*
Investire,	*To invest.*
Investatio,	*An Investing.*
Jocalia,	*Jewels.*
Irrotulare,	*To enrol.*
Irrotulatio,	*An Enrolling.*
Irrotulamentum,	*An Enrolment.*
Junctura,	*A Jointure.*
Jurata,	*A Jury.*

K.

KAIA,	*A Quay.*
Kaiagium,	*Quayage.*
Kidellus,	*A Wear.*

L.

LABORARIUS,	*A Labourer.*
Landa vel Launda,	*A Land or Open Field.*
Lasta,	*A Last.*
Lesura,	*A Leasowe.*
Leta,	*A Leet.*
Levabilis,	*Leviable.*
Levella,	*A Level.*
Libellus,	*A Libel.*
Librata,	*A Pound Weight.*
Liberatura, Liberata,	*A Livery.*
Ligeus,	*A Liege-man.*
Ligeancia,	*Allegiance.*
Lista,	*A List.*
Logia, Lodgia,	*A Lodge.*
Loppatus,	*Lopped.*

M.

MAEREMIUM,	*Timber.*
Mahemium,	*A Maim.*
Mahemiare, Mutilare,	*To maim.*
Manerium,	*A Manor.*
Domus Manerialis,	*A Manor-House.*
Mansum, Mansura,	*A Dwelling.*
Manutenere,	*To maintain.*
Manutenentia,	*Maintenance.*
Manutentor,	*A Maintainer.*
Marcare,	*To take by Reprisal.*
Marchiare,	*To march.*

Marchie

Marchie Wallie,	The Marches of Wales.
Marlera, Marlia,	} Marle.
Terra Marlanda, vel Melioranda,	} Marled Land.
Masca,	A Masque.
Medius, mesne,	Mean.
Menialis serviens,	A menial Servant.
Memorandum,	Be it remembered.
Memoranda,	Remembrances.
Menestrallus,	A Minstrel.
Mera,	A Meer.
Mercatum,	A Market.
Mercator,	A Merchant.
Mercandiza,	Merchandize.
Mercimonia,	Wares.
Mercatura,	Trading.
Mercandizare,	To trade.
Merceria,	Mercery.
Mercerus,	A Mercer.
Messuagium,	A Messuage.
Minera,	A Mine.
Minetarius, Minerarius,	} A Miner.
Mise, vel Misis.	Costs.
Misprisitio,	Misprision.
Misterium,	A Mystery, a Trade.
Mixtilio,	{ Maslin, or Meslin, Wheat, and Rye.
Mora,	Moorish Ground.
Morina,	The Murrain.
Morsellatim,	By Morsels.
Mortgagium,	A Mortgage.
Morganizandum,	To mortgage.
Mossa,	A Moss.
Mossetum,	Mossy Ground.
Multura, Mulctura,	} Toll for Grist of a Mill.
Murdrum,	Murder.
Marditor.	A Murderer.
Murderare,	To murder.
Mustrum,	A Muster.
Mustratio,	Mustering.

N.

NIMIETAS ponderis,	} Too much Weight.
Noca terre, vel Noka terre,	} A Nook of Land.
Noctuatim,	Nightly, Night by Night.

O.

ORA,	An Oar.
Oviele,	A Sheepwalk.

P.

PACCUM Mercerie,	A Pack of Mercery Wares.
Comitatus Palatinus,	A County Palatine.
Palus,	A Pale.
Palicium Parci,	Park Pales.
Palmata,	A Handful.
Panellum Juratorum,	A Panel of Jurors.
Pandoxator,	A Brewer.
Pandoxatorium,	A Brewhouse.
Parcellare,	To parcel out.
Parcus,	A Park or Pound.
Parcarius,	The Keeper of a Park.
Pardonare,	To pardon.
Pardonatio,	A Pardon.
Passare,	To pass.
Passagium,	A Passage.
Passagium ultra agnam,	} A Ferry.
Pasturatio, Depasturatio,	} A Pasturing.
Pasturare, depasturare,	To depasture.
Pavilo,	A Pavilion.
Pegasus,	A Post-Horse.
Performare,	To perform.
Performatio,	A Performance.
Perquirere,	To purchase.
Perquisitio, Perquisitum,	} A Purchase.
Perquisitor,	A Purchaser.
Pertinentia,	An Appurtenance.
Pertinentijs,	Appurtenances.
Picagium,	Picage.
Pightellum,	A Pightel of Land.
Pillorium, Pilloria,	} A Pillory.
Pipa de Allome,	A Pipe of Alum.
Placea Terre,	A Place of Land.
Placea Prati,	A Place of Meadow.
Placea Bosci,	A Place of Wood.
Placitare,	To plead.
Placitum,	A Plea.
Placitatio,	Pleading.
Platea,	A Street.
Plegius,	A Surety, a Pledge.
Plegiagium, Plegiatio,	} Suretyship.

Contra

Contra Vadium &}	*Against Sureties and*
Plegium, }	*Pledges.*
Plevina,	*Plevin, Replevin.*
Pola,	*A Pole or Perch.*
Pondaginm,	*Poundage.*
Pontagium,	*Pontage.*
Porteria,	*The Place of Porter.*
Portgrevius,	*A Portrieve.*
Postdisseisina,	*Post-disseisin.*
Potagium,	*Pottage.*
Practizare,	*To practise.*
Prebenda,	*A Prebend.*
Prebendarius,	*A Prebendary.*
Prebenda,	*Provender.*
Precaria,	*A Day's Work.*
Preferamentum,	*Preferment.*
Preferencia,	*Preference.*
Præfictitio diei,	{ *The Prefixion or Assigning of a Day.*
Prelacia,	*Prelacy.*
Presidens,	*A President.*
PrepositusPrepositure {	*The Provost of a Provostship, 2 H. 5, 9.*
Prepositus Villæ, vel Prepositi Villarum, {	*The Principal Man or Men of the Town or Towns, Village or Villages.*
Prerogativa,	*Prerogative.*
Prescriptio,	*Prescription.*
Presbyteratus,	*Presbytery.*
Prisa,	{ *A Drift of Cattle depasturing in a Common.*
Prisagium,	*Prise or Taking.*
Principalium,	*An Heir-Loom.*
Prisona,	*A Prison.*
Prisonarius,	*A Prisoner.*
Imprisonamentum,	*Imprisonment.*
Proditionaliter,	*Treasonably.*
Propars,	} *A Purparty of Lands held by Parceners.*
Propartia.	
Proportionabilis,	*Proportionable.*
Proportionare,	*To proportion.*
Prorogatio,	*A Prorogation.*
Prorogatus,	*Prorogued.*
Prostrare,	*To throw down.*
Proviso,	*Provided.*
Pulletria,	*Poultry.*
Computatorium in Pulletria,	} *The Poultry Compter.*
Purportans,	*Purporting*
Purporta,	*A Purport.*
Purprestura,	*A Purpresture.*
Purprisa,	} *A Purprise.*
Purprisum,	

Q.

QUARENTENA Terre,	} *A Quarentine, a Quantity of Land of 40 Perches.*
Quarentena Mulieris,	{ *Woman's Quarentine. See the Stat. of Merton.*
Quareria,	*A Quarry.*
Quo minus potuerunt,	{ *So that they could not, or might the less.*

R.

RATA, Ratum,	*A Rate.*
Ratihabitio,	*A Confirmation.*
Receptamentum,	{ *A Receiving, Entertaining, or Harbouring.*
Receptare,	*To receive.*
Rechasiare,	*To drive forth again.*
Recognitio,	*A Recognizance.*
Recognitor,	*A Conusor.*
Recognoscere,	} *To try.*
Recognitura,	
Recompensare,	*To recompense.*
Recompensatio,	*A Recompence.*
Rectatus,	} *Charged with an Offence.*
Arrectatus,	
Retrum rectatus,	*Again charged.*
Redisseisina,	*Redisseisin.*
Refeoffare,	*To reinfeoff.*
Refullum Aque,	*An Overflow of Water.*
Regalia,	*Royalties.*
Regardum,	} *A Reward.*
Rewardum,	
Regardum Foreste,	} *A Regard of a Forest.*
Rewardum Foreste,	
Regardans,	*Regarding.*
Registrarius,	*A Register.*
Registrum,	*The Register.*
Regratarius,	*A Regrator.*
Remanere,	*Remainder.*
Remaneribus,	*Remainders.*
Dare ad Remanentiam,	} *To give in perpetuity.*
Remediare,	*To remedy.*
Remembrancia,	*A Remembrance.*
Rengi Stamellorum carnificum,	} *Ranges of Butchers' Stalls.*
Rentale,	*A Rental.*
Repassagium,	*Repassage.*
Repellum,	*A Repeal.*
Repellatio,	*A Repealing.*
Repellatus,	*Repealed.*

K   *Replegiare.*

Replegiare, Replegiamentum,	} A Replevin.
Replegiari,	To be reprieved.
Reportare,	To report.
Reportus,	A Report.
Reprisa,	A Reprise, a Deduction.
Reprisale,	A Reprisal.
Residentia, Resiantia, Reseantisa.	} Residence.
Residere,	To reside.
Rescussus,	A Rescue.
Resortare,	To resort.
Resortiebatur jus,	{ The Right of Resort, as from Uncle to Nephew.
Restaurus Equorum,	{ A Breed or Store of Horses. See Stauras.
Retallium, Retallia,	} Retail.
Retinentia,	A Retinue.
Retirare,	To retire.
Retornare,	To return.
Retornum,	A Return.
Revella,	Revels.
Riflura,	Rifling.
Riga,	A Ridge.
Rinn,	A Rhine.
Riottum, Riotum,	} A Riot.
Riotose & routouse,	Riotously and routously.
Riparia,	{ The Bank of a River, or the River itself.
Roba,	A Robe.
Robaria, Roberia,	} A Robbery.
Robbator,	A Robber.
Roberatores.	Robbers.
Rogus,	A Rogue.
Romea,	A Room.
Rotulus,	A Roll.
Irrotulare,	To enrol.
Routum,	{ A Rout, or unlawful Assembly.
Rossinum,	Rosin.
Rubbosa,	Rubbish.
Russetum,	Russet.
Russatorum pannorum.	Russet Cloths.

S.

SALSARIUM,	A Saltseller.
Sappum, Succus,	Juice or Sap.

Scarletum,	Scarlet.
Scavaginm,	Scavage—a Kind of Toll.
Scire facere,	To cause to know.
Scituatus, Scitus,	} Situated.
Scitus,	A Scite.
Scota, Scotare,	} A Scot, To scot, { An ancient mode of Taxation by Scot and Lot.
Scutaginm,	Escuage or Shield-Money.
Seasonabile tempus, vel tempus Seisonis,	} Seasonable Time.
Sectare,	To sue.
Secta,	A Suit.
Secta Molendini,	Suit of a Mill.
Secta Shirorum,	Shire Suit.
Secta, vel Sewettum Prisone,	} Prison Suit.
Secta ad Curiam,	Suit to a Court.
Securare,	To secure.
Securantia,	An Assurance.
Scisina,	Seisin.
Scisitus,	Seised.
Seisire,	To seize.
Disseisina,	A Disseisin.
Postdisseisina,	A Post Disseisin.
Selda,	A Stall, Shed, or Shop.
Shopa, sive Selda,	A Shop or Shed.
Selio,	A Sation of Land.
Se moventia,	Things moving alone.
Sententiare,	To sentence.
Seperalis,	Several.
Sequestrare,	To sequester.
Sequestrum, Sequestratio,	} A Sequestering.
Serviens ad legem,	A Serjeant at Law.
Sewera,	A Sewer.
Shippare,	To ship.
Shira,	A Shire.
Signetum, vel Signettum Regis,	} The King's Signet.
Siligo,	Rye.
Simulcom, Unacum,	} Together with.
Soca,	A Soke.
Socagium,	Socage.
Solarium, vel Sollatrium,	} A Solar, or Upper Room. a Garret.
Soldarius,	A Soldier.
Solicitator,	A Solicitor.
Stalla, Stallum,	} A Stall.
Stallagium,	Stallage.

Standards,

Standarda.	
Standardum.	} A Standard.
Stapula.	} A Staple for Wares.
Stapulum.	
Statutum Stapule,	Statute of the Staple.
Staurus,	A Store or Stock.
Stieca, vel Sticens Anguillarum,	} A Stick of Eels.
Straminari,	To be covered with Straw.
Strata,	A Street.
Stubula,	Stubble.
Stuffura,	Stuffing.
Subbosens,	Underwood growing.
Breve de Subpœnæ,	A Writ of Subpœna.
Suera, vel Sewera,	A Sewer.
Summaginm,	An Horse-Load.
Superedificium.	An Over Building.
Supertunica,	An Upper Coat.
Supervisor,	A Surveyor.
Supervisus,	A Survey.
Surplusagium,	Surplusage.

T.

TALLAGIUM,	Tallage.
Tallin,	A Tally.
Tallium,	An Entail.
Talliare,	To entail.
Tamdiu, quamdiu,	As long as.
Tannarius,	A Tanner.
Tannare,	To tan.
Tannaria,	A Tanner's Craft.
Tappa,	A Tap.
Opere Tapitiarij,	Upholsterers' Work.
Tastare vinum,	To taste Wine.
Tassum,	A Cock or Heap of Hay.
Tassari,	To make into Cocks.
Fenum in Tassis,	Hay in Cocks.
Taxa,	A Tax.
Taxatio,	A Taxing.
Taxatores,	Assessors of Taxes.
Tenentia,	A Tenancy.
Tenura, Tenatura, Tentio,	} A Tenure or Holding.
Tentoria Mercatoria,	Merchants' Tents.
Terminarius,	A Termor or Lessee.
Terraria,	Terriers.
Territorium,	A Territory.
Theolonium,	Toll.
Thesauraria, Domus Thesauraria,	} A Treasure-house.

Tillagium,	Tillage.
Minera Tinnei,	A Mine of Tin.
Domus Tipularia,	{ A Tippling-house or Alehouse.
Tithinga,vel Decenna,	A Tything.
Todda,	A Tod of Wool.
Toftum,	A Toft.
Tolnetum,	A Toll.
Tolta,	A Toll.
Tonna,	A Ton.
Tonnagium,	Tonnage.
Topare arbores,	To top Trees.
Torcherus, vel Torticius,	} A Torch.
Tortum facere,	To do wrong.
Tracea,	A Trace or Tract.
Ex transverso Ripe,	Cross the Bank.
――――――Vie,	―――― Way.
――――――Vallis,	―――――Valley.
――――――Aque,	――――Water.
Trava Baldi,	A Thrave of Corn.
Traversia,	A Traverse.
Trenchea, Trenchia,	} A Trench.
Tressoria, vel Trestoria Mulierum,	} Women's Tressels.
Triare,	To try.
Triatio,	A Trial.
Triator,	A Trier.
Trimestre Spacium,	Three Months' Space.
Tumbrellum,	A Tumbrel.
Turba,	A Turf.
Turbaria,	Turbary.
Communia Turbariæ, vel Turbagium,	} Common of Turbary.
Turnum Vicecomitis,	The Sheriff's Turn.

V.

VACCARIA,	A Cowhouse.
Vadium,	Suretyship or Security.
Vadius,	A Surety.
Vadiare,	To wage; as
Vadiare Legem, vel	To wage Law:
Liberationem Averiorum,	} To deliver Cattle distrained.
Vadium,	Wages, Vails.
Valectus, Valetus, Valettus,	} A Groom.
Valentia,	Value.
	Valibilis,

Valibilis,	Valuable.
Vastum,	Waste.
Velvettum,	Velvet.
Venaria Parci,	The Game of a Park.
Venella,	A Lane.
Ventriticum, Molendinum,	} A Windmill.
Vervices,	Wether Sheep.
Veredictum,	A Verdict.
Verificare,	To aver.
Verificatio,	An Averment.
Vestura,	{ The Grass or Herbage of Land.
Vestura Terræ,	{ The Crop or Profits of Land.
Vestitura Bosci.	The Profits of Wood.
Viagium,	A Voyage.
Vicinetum,	The Neighbourhood.
Victualarius, Vitellarius,	} A Victualler.
Victualia,	Victuals.
Viculus,	A Little Street.
Villula,	A Little Village.
Vintenarius,	A Vintner.
Viridarius,	A Verderer of the Forest.
Virgatores,	Vergers.
Vivarium,	A Fish-Pond or Warren.

U.

UMPIRATOR.	An Umpire.
Unciata,	A Ounce Weight.
Ura Plumbea,	Lead Ore.
Usagium,	An Usage.
Utlagare,	To outlaw.
Utlagaria,	An Outlawry.
Utterare,	To utter.

W.

WAGA,	A Weigh.
Waiviaria,	A Waiver.
Femina Waiviata,	A Woman waived.
Waivium,	A Waif.
Bona Waiviata,	Goods waived.
Wallia, Wallensica,	} Wales.
Wallia,	A Wall.
Wallatur Fossato,	Inclosed by a Ditch.
Wapentagium,	A Wapentake.
Warrantizare,	To warrant.
Warrantia,	A Warranty.
Warda,	A Ward in the City.
Warda Castri,	Castle Guard.
Warrantum,	A Warrant.
Warrectum,	Fallow Land.
Tempus warrectandi,	Time of fallowing.
Terra jacens frisca & ad Warrectum,	} Land lying fresh and fallow.
Warenna,	A Warren.
Warennarius,	A Warrener.
Wharfa,	A Wharf.
Walda, vel Wilda Sussexie,	} The Wold or Wild of Sussex.
Woodwardus,	A Woodward.
Wreccum,	Wreck.
Bona Wreccata,	Goods wrecked.

Y.

YARDA,	A Yard. Co. Ent. 377.

FINIS.

LONDON:—STRANGEWAYS and WALDEN, Printers, 28 Castle St. Leicester Sq.